I wanted to share with you how much your book is helping me. It is giving me a sense of belonging, understanding, forgiveness and acceptance. Thank you deeply.

—Karina Hadida

Indigo Adults

Indigo Adults

✦

Forerunners of the New Civilization

*Are You a Grown-Up Indigo Soul
and Don't Know It?*

*Kabir Jaffe
and
Ritama Davidson*

iUniverse, Inc.
New York Lincoln Shanghai

Indigo Adults
Forerunners of the New Civilization

Copyright © 2005 by Kabir Jaffe

iUniverse books may be ordered through booksellers or by contacting:

iUniverse
2021 Pine Lake Road, Suite 100
Lincoln, NE 68512
www.iuniverse.com
1-800-Authors (1-800-288-4677)

ISBN-13: 978-0-595-36692-7 (pbk)
ISBN-13: 978-0-595-81115-1 (ebk)
ISBN-10: 0-595-36692-9 (pbk)
ISBN-10: 0-595-81115-9 (ebk)

Printed in the United States of America

To the New Humanity

Contents

Acknowledgements

We would like to thank all the people who have helped to make this book possible.

Our parents, for the wonderful jobs they did in helping us keep in touch with our Indigo Nature.

The participants in our trainings who have taught us the most about Indigo's.

Our team at the center in Germany who provided the support system for these talks to happen.

Rikta Butler for her encouragement, ideas and for transcribing the talks.

Solange de Marignac for her support in helping in the production of this book.

The many friends who have given us feedback along the way as we produced the book.

And a special thanks to our team in Argentina who so enthusiastically produced the first version of this book in Spanish.

Preface

A new type of person is coming into incarnation right now, almost a 'next step' as humanity progresses. These people hold great hope for the future—the promise of a new humanity and civilization. They carry different energies, paradigms, ways of thinking and feeling. These new people are called 'Indigo Souls' because clairvoyants notice that the color indigo is unusually prominent in their aura. Indigo is the color seen in the third eye; these souls have a high degree of activity in their third eye center. Though we could as easily have referred to these souls as 'the new souls', 'Aquarian souls', or other such names that are currently being used, we felt that 'Indigo' addressed the fundamental differences in their energetic and psychological makeup.

In our work leading seminars on self-development around the world, we come across thousands of Indigo Souls. Most of them are already adults, but very few know they are Indigo or understand their soul nature. Many are struggling because they are different. They frequently feel alone, separate or misunderstood. They have a depth of feeling and thinking that differs from those around them. They have powerful internal forces of energy, intelligence, and feeling that they often don't understand, and consequently find difficult to manage. They are unusually sensitive, making them more easily disturbed by things that don't bother others. They carry aspirations and visions which make them long for something more, and be dissatisfied with the world as it is. They often feel limited and frustrated by what is considered the 'normal world' around.

If the above description speaks to you, then you are probably an Indigo Soul. This book contains the understandings and discoveries we have made as we wrestled with our nature as Indigo Adults as well as through our work with others. We hope these materials will be as valuable to you as they have been to us, and will help you understand more clearly who you are, what you carry within you, and your purpose as an Indigo Soul here on Earth.

The material for this book was developed by both of us, and was then given as a series of eight evening lectures by Kabir in Frankfurt, Germany, over the spring and summer of 2003. The format was a lecture followed by questions and answers. Chapter One was a later addition and does not contain questions.

This book starts with a short section on astrology. We realize that many readers may not be interested in or knowledgeable about astrology, and that some may be actively resistant to it. Bear with us for just a short while. We think it will be worth it. Our experience is that astrology brings an important key to understanding the Indigo phenomenon.

This book is rooted in our personal experience of the subtle dimension of life, and also reflects our explorations into the esoteric and mystic teachings of many traditions. Our work is focused upon the human energy system—the energy field surrounding the body and the energy centers within it. This energy perspective is reflected throughout the book and in the structure of the book itself—chapters 6-8 being based on the unfoldment of the Indigo energies through the seven energy centers.

We recognize that the subtle dimension of life is not so tangible to our 'normal' analytic mind, and it is only beginning to be documented by scientific proof. Take what we are presenting as a hypothesis. Experiment with it, and come to your own conclusions.

1

What are Indigo Souls?

What are Indigo Souls?
Why is the Indigo phenomenon happening?

To understand Indigo Souls it is helpful to know a little about astrological cycles—the 'bigger picture' of unfolding time.

We are all intimately familiar with astrology: the rhythms of day and night and the cycle of the seasons—the phases of life created by the movement of the celestial bodies. The seasons particularly exemplify the essence of astrology: growth, flowering, decay, and quiescence.

This seasonal cycle is broken down into twelve phases of development, each phase being represented as one of the zodiacal signs. The cycle starts with the sign Aries—the first day of spring—representing beginnings, birth, and emergence. The cycle then progresses around the zodiac through Taurus, Gemini, Cancer, etc., to end with the sign of Pisces, representing ending, completion, and return.

There is an even larger cycle at work than the yearly seasonal cycle. It is called the Great Year. It is formed by the precession of the equinoxes, and creates a cycle of 25,920 years. Because of complex celestial mechanics, the first day of spring, the spring equinox, slowly moves backwards (precession) around the zodiac by one astrological sign every 2160 years. This 2160-year period we call an Age, i.e., the Age of Pisces, the Age of Aquarius, etc.

About 2000 years ago the first day of spring was aligned with the meeting point of Aries and Pisces. This meeting point is called a cusp[1]. Since then, the first day of spring has been moving backwards through the sign of Pisces. It is for this reason that the past 2000 years is referred to as the Piscean Age.

Why is this important? The best analogy is to imagine the signs of the zodiac as celestial lenses, each lens having a particular coloring. When the Earth is

---

1. This is an approximate beginning point. The exact degree of the beginnings of the signs is not known. The cusp period lasts a couple of hundred years.

aligned with a particular lens, for example Pisces, then the energies of Pisces flow into the Earth sphere. To help understand how these energy streams affect the Earth, you can think of the full moon. When we are under a full moon, it affects the waters of the planet and we have our highest tides. The full moon affects us personally too. Sometimes we can't sleep well, or our emotions are stimulated. In a similar way the energies of an astrological Age influence our planet and our psyches.

Each Age creates its own 'mood'. It brings to the foreground certain archetypal images, beliefs, and paradigms, and stimulates certain chakras[2] within the human energy field with their corresponding thoughts, emotions, and behaviors. The energies of an Age are an immensely powerful force shaping our lives in countless ways; the psychology of the peoples of that Age, the form of religion and spirituality, the structure of society and the very fabric of civilization.

Let's look at some examples. The Arian Age (the Age that came before Pisces, approximately 2160 B.C.—0 A.D.) was characterized by the sign Aries (the Ram), and the planet Mars. Aries carries the energies of assertion, initiation, expansion, will, and war. (It is associated with and stimulates some of the qualities of the first or base chakra—aggression, and some of the qualities of the third or solar plexus chakra—domination, power, and conquest.) The Arian Age was an age of empire, war, and expansion. It was dominated by Mars, the god of war, and the symbol for male virility. The energies of an Age are exemplified in its symbols and myths. Some of the gods of the Arian Age were the warlike Marduk of Babylon and the wrathful Yahweh of the Old Testament. The development of the Roman Kingdom (753 B.C.) exemplifies the energies of this period.

We are most familiar with the Piscean energies of the last 2000 years as our current civilization and psyche are still so highly influenced by them. The birth of Christianity is the 'event' which ushered in the Piscean Age and has colored this past 2000 years. The symbol of the sign Pisces is the Fish. The two tails of the fish were the early symbol of Christianity. And the Christ, suffering for humanity on the cross, is a powerful symbol of the Piscean themes of sacrifice, suffering, redemption, and transcendence.

Pisces is a water sign. Water is the element of feelings and emotions. Pisces is connected to religion and spirituality (operating through the seventh or crown chakra), the basic emotions connected to family and to our inner child (the sec-

---

2.   The word chakra comes from Sanskrit and is used to refer to one of the seven energy centers within the human energy system. We will use both the word chakra and center throughout the book to describe these energetic vortexes.

ond or sacral chakra), and the heart, connected with love and compassion (the fourth or heart chakra). The result of the Piscean influence has been to turn the focus of humanity towards love, spirituality and the 'other world' in an emotional and innocent, or childlike way. The influence of Pisces has been a major step on the evolutionary journey of humanity. It began to shift the energies from the war-like mode of the Arian Age towards love and forgivingness, as exemplified by Jesus and his teachings. It has changed the old mode of an eye for an eye to a new understanding of turning the other cheek and loving your neighbor as you would love yourself.

The emotional nature of Pisces has created an emotional/devotional approach to spirit. It has emphasized feeling-based communion and the attitudes of belief and faith, rather than understanding. It is a sign of service and sacrifice, compassion and forgivingness, keynotes of the Christian era. But Pisces is also a sign of self-denial and personal condemnation (mea culpa), in which suffering is seen as a way to cleanse our soul, and our personal joy in this life should be sacrificed for eternal happiness in the after-world.

The Energies of Aquarius

At this moment we are in the meeting point of Pisces and Aquarius. The energies of Aquarius are starting to penetrate the Earth. Although they are beginning to be felt, it is only a beginning, and the Piscean energies are still the dominant 'note'. This is because of two reasons—first, we still exist in the Piscean structure of civilization which has been built over the last 2000 years—and second, the Pisces energies, though waning, are still flowing on to the Earth.

At the same time, we have a steadily increasing inflow of energies from Aquarius, bringing new paradigms, ways of thought, feeling, and behavior. The cusp is a transition between the old and the new. Two Ages are meeting. Both energies are present—it is a dynamic and exciting time.

What is Aquarius bringing? Some of its keynotes are freedom, progressiveness, individuality, intellectual understanding, and group consciousness. We first began to feel these Aquarian energies on the planet when the spring equinox entered the cusp between Pisces and Aquarius, roughly in the 1700s.

Every Age begins with one or more keynote events which 'strike the cord' of the themes and energies for that Age. The formation of the United States, with its constitutional basis of freedom of speech and religion, and its structure of many individual states joined together in a common union, is one of the powerful symbols for the themes of this coming Age.

Aquarius is an air sign. Air is the element of the mind. Aquarius works primarily through the third eye (the sixth chakra) at the center of the forehead. This chakra has to do with two levels of our intelligence—the analytic mind and the intuition. The increased stimulation of the third eye through the incoming Aquarian energies is awakening in humanity a new level of mental activity, understanding, and intuition into the subtle worlds.

It is this opening of the third eye that is one of the main underlying causes of the many developments we have seen in society over the last couple of centuries. Let me emphasize this point. Imagine that the energies of an Age come in and stimulate specific centers in the human psyche. The activity of these centers creates a new level of thought and behavior that then externalizes as culture and civilization. An Age emerges from inside of us and then gets expressed outwards.

The Industrial Revolution, then the discovery of electricity (electricity is ruled by the sign of Aquarius), and now the emergence of the information age, are the result of the new capacities of intelligent thought that are emerging through our third eye.

This stimulation of the third eye and the mind creates a fundamentally different psychology in the Aquarian person, a psychology based upon an increased activity of the mind. We have a new level of intellectual activity and one of its most potent manifestations is our desire to understand. Our minds are questing. We want to know. The average person in the First World can read and write, uses a computer, and lives in a world of technological and scientific marvels. We approach life not only with feeling but also with the mind. We don't believe because someone tells us to; we want information, facts, reasons, and proof. And we want the freedom to make our own informed decisions.

This capacity of intelligence is not the only capacity that is unfolding through the third eye. The third eye has two aspects, referred to as 'petals.' The lower petal holds the analytical mind with its faculty of intelligent thought and reasoning. It is this petal that is responsible for the qualities of intelligence mentioned above. The upper petal holds what is commonly called the intuition. We use the word 'intuition' in a particular way. It refers to another sense apparatus that gives us the ability to tune to a subtle world of energy, thought, and feeling.

Most of us are familiar with the use of the word intuition in a more down-to-earth sense, like a mother's intuition. But there is another level as well. We are speaking here of a type of intuition that is connected to a higher knowing, to a spiritual type of knowledge. This type of intuition perceives in terms of larger gestalts and interrelationships that exist within and around us. It's connected to a higher mental capacity that has to do with Beingness and the Soul. Is from here that insight comes, often as an unexpected flash of clarity or illumination, and from here that genius draws its inspiration.

Another facet of this intuitive capacity is the ability to self-reflect. It is through the upper petal of the third eye that we can examine our own thoughts and feelings. Now this may not sound like much. Anyone can easily say, "Of course I can examine my own thoughts and feelings. I know when I'm angry, sad, or happy. What's the big deal?"

But this something more. It's the ability to look deeper into our feelings, to sense the subtle nuances, and to understand our deeper psychological motivations. We can trace what appears to be a momentary feeling back in time to our past, to our childhood upbringing, perhaps even further. We can see how this feeling or pattern may have been passed down to us from our grandparents or our great grandparents, or perhaps even from previous incarnations. This ability to self-reflect at these depths is a new type of thinking that has only recently emerged on a widespread level. Its emergence within our psyche has given birth to the field of psychology, and to the widespread interest in self-development.

Another aspect of the upper petal is the need to find higher meaning and significance. We live for values and purpose. We have a sophisticated worldview, a weltanschauung, in which we perceive our interrelationship with the larger whole, and we seek to find our place and make our contribution. We begin to recognize that there is a great interweaving of life—that we are not separate individuals, but are rather part of an interwoven fabric of energy. We see that each part is related to every other part and that everything affects everything else.

It is the inflowing energies of Aquarius and their stimulation of the upper petal of the third eye that is one of the primary forces creating what is commonly called the New Age movement. If you think about it, the New Age movement is the reflection of our emerging capacity to look more deeply at ourselves, our desires to know who we really are, our explorations into the subtle forces of psychology, energy, the soul, and spirit, and our awareness of our interrelationship with the larger whole.

The Indigo Soul Group

Each astrological age brings in not only the energies of that sign, which then play upon the planet, but it also brings in a specific group of souls. What this means is that there are different soul groups, each group aligned or associated with a particular sign. There was a soul group that was part of the Piscean Age and carried the Piscean energies. This was the group that was primarily in incarnation during the Piscean Age. Now as the Aquarian Age comes in, we have the Aquarian energies playing upon the planet and the Aquarian soul group coming into incarnation.

The Aquarian Soul group that is incarnating now has significant differences from the Piscean soul group. They have different activities in their chakras with the resultant differences in psychology, thought, feeling, and behavior.

These souls first began to incarnate in the 1700s. At that time there was only a trickle of them. They incarnated into a Piscean culture and civilization, carrying new ideas and energies that were very different than what was then the norm. In a sense these individuals seeded the Piscean culture with Aquarian energies. They were the first faint green shoots of what, over centuries, will grow into full bloom.

Indigo Soul Time Line

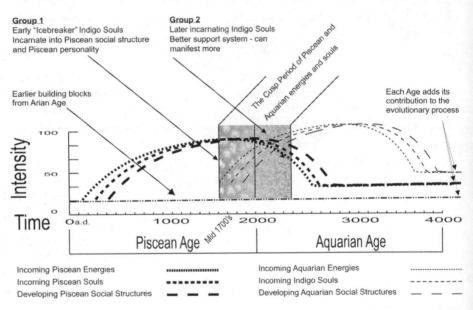

Diagram 1-1

Diagram 1-1

Indigo Soul Time Line

The Unfoldment of an Age
An Age begins with an inflow of new energies. Shortly after, souls connected with that sign begin to incarnate. These souls bring new ideas and ways of living that gradually create changes in the structure and organization of society.

The Meeting of Two Ages
As a new age starts coming in the previous age begins to wane. During this period, called the cusp, both ages are present. Two great streams of energy are meeting. It is a time of cultures in collision.

Group 1
Indigo energies and Souls began coming onto the planet around the early 1700s. These early incarnators have the toughest job of 'breaking the ice' and bringing in the first of the new energies. They have ushered in the industrial revolution, electricity, scientific thought, and the new ideals of liberty and freedom.

Group 2
We are now in a culture in transition, and it is a time of sweeping change. Something new has been born within you and within the culture. This became especially obvious with the new spirit that emerged in the 1960s. But there is still much struggle as we wrestle with the outer layers of our personality and the outer establishment, both of which still carry much of the old.

We stand today between two Ages

This brings us to where we are today. We exist in the cusp period between two ages. On the one hand we have the Piscean Age, which has externalized and crystallized an entire civilization with its institutions, religions, organizations, cultures, and ways of being. And on the other hand, we have the incoming Aquarian energies and the corresponding soul group, what we are calling Indigo, coming into incarnation in greater and greater numbers and gradually unfolding what will in time become the next culture and civilization.

So we have two radically different forces at work today: an established Age with a crystallized planetary culture that is in decline, and a new and very small minority of people and ideas that are the first seeds of what will become the next Age. An interesting moment to be alive! And a very interesting moment if you are an Indigo Soul carrying the new energies.

It was only recently (the past 10 years or so) that the Indigo phenomena gained public attention. It began because schools and parents were noticing a growing number of children who were 'different'. These kids were highly individual, rebellious, very intelligent, and didn't fit the established school system. They had unusually fast minds that moved at a different pace than that of normal kids (the attention deficit disorder syndrome). They had a different spirit, way of relating, and sense of who they were.

A psychic observing these children coined the name 'Indigo Children' to describe them because of the indigo color in their aura. The color of the third eye is indigo. In these children the third eye is highly active, and the color indigo radiates from the third eye and colors their entire aura.

Since then, the idea of Indigo Children has become more known, particularly through the book 'The Indigo Children' by Lee Carroll and Jan Tober. Some of the most advanced of these children, those with exceptional psychic gifts and wisdom, have become the symbols of this new generation. Many parents wonder if their child is an Indigo child, and a few school systems have begun to find ways to educate this new generation.

In our seminars, we realized that there were already a very large number of Indigo Souls in incarnation who were already adults. Most had grown up invisibly, meaning nobody had noticed they were different. Most of these adults (and most Indigo Children too) were bright, but didn't have the exceptional psychic gifts that are commonly associated with Indigos. And because they didn't stand out as exceptionally gifted individuals, they tended to go unnoticed.

It is these adults who were the majority of the participants in our workshops. They knew they were different, but they didn't know why, what it meant, how to handle it, or what they were supposed to do with it. Many of them had suffered a great deal because of this—they felt different, separate, alone, and misunderstood. Many of them felt there was something wrong with them because they didn't fit, with the resultant feelings of inferiority, self-judgment, etc. What a strange and painful thing: people who were so beautiful and carried such potentials of the new, yet were struggling so deeply. These people have a deep need to understand themselves. What is their inner process? How can they be supported?

It is not easy being an Indigo Adult. Indigo Adults have incarnated into the denser vibrations of the Piscean Age and have been breaking the ground and planting the first seeds of the Aquarian civilization. Their job is hard. They have incarnated into an environment which does not support them, and in many ways actively tries to shut them down. They have grown up in families and been educated by school systems, which have conditioned them with the Piscean ways, and not supported the Aquarian/Indigo spirit hidden within them. The result is that many of them have become, on the surface—in their outer personality and ways of thinking, feeling, and behaving—primarily Piscean, with only a small level of the Indigo energies showing. Yet they carry a deeper Indigo spirit underneath. We call this state the Indigo Soul in the Piscean Personality. This is not easy (See Indigo Soul in Piscean Personality diagram).

The more recent Indigo Children and some of the Indigo Adults, especially those who incarnated to parents who themselves are Indigos, have it easier. First of all, the times are already less dense. And these parents are supporting their children's Indigo nature and putting less Piscean conditioning on them. Their personality reflects more of the new and is more aligned with the qualities of their Indigo souls. We refer to them as Indigo Souls living in Indigo Personalities.

Indigo Souls in Piscean Personalties

The Past

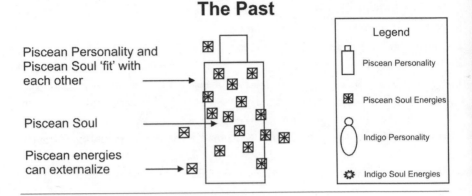

Piscean Personality and Piscean Soul 'fit' with each other

Piscean Soul

Piscean energies can externalize

Legend

Piscean Personality

Piscean Soul Energies

Indigo Personality

Indigo Soul Energies

The Present

Some areas of the personality carry Indigo energies

But most are Piscean

Piscean Personality has become stiff and rigid after being established for 2000 years

Indigo Soul Within

Internal friction between old and new

Not easy to externalize what is inside

The Future

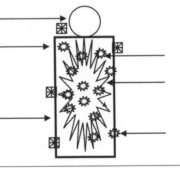

Indigo Soul

Greater internal harmony because an Indigo Soul is in an Indigo Personality

Indigo Personality reflects the new and is more fluid and flexible

More of the Indigo Soul can come through and externalize

Diagram 1-2

Diagram 1-2

The Past—Piscean Souls in a Piscean Personality Structure
Over the past 2000 years, the Piscean Age has formed the Piscean personality type and built a Piscean culture and civilization. The Piscean Soul is integral within the Piscean Personality. It is in balance and 'right' in its time.

The Present—Indigo Souls in a composite Piscean/Indigo Personality Structure
Towards the end of the Piscean Age the energies become crystallized, institutionalized and entrenched. This is the environment Indigo's arrive in to. The Indigo Soul comes in to a family and is brought up in a school and religious system which is primarily Piscean. These influences shape their outer personality structure even while their inner consciousness is Indigo. This causes a discrepancy and an internal clash between the Indigo soul within and the primarily Piscean-dominated personality which lets through a little of the Indigo energies.

The Future—Indigo Souls in an Indigo Personality Structure
Some of the Indigo children today, many of whom have been born to Indigo parents, are more integrated, being Indigo Souls with Indigo personality structures. They can express more of their Aquarian nature. And these children are still only an early step. As the outer society becomes more Aquarian it will allow more of the Indigo nature to express. We have only just begun to see the qualities of these new souls.

2

The Changing of an Age

An age begins with the birth of ideas. New ideals enter the collective consciousness, and new possibilities of living and relating begin to emerge. New aspects of the psyche begin to show themselves, like the petals of a flower previously hidden in the bud, now becoming visible. New social structures are seeded, to later take shape as social institutions. Discoveries in different areas, economic, scientific, or social emerge to gradually have widespread effects.

What is born at the beginning of an age creates an evolution in civilization. In the early phases the energies are youthful. They are new and fresh, vital and alive. The ideas and understandings are in a 'pure' form. They are often idealistic, perhaps not yet realistic, but they speak of possibilities that move us.

Over a period of 2000 years these energies are slowly 'enculturated,' or built into the fabric of the culture. Over time these ideas crystallize into established thought and behavioral patterns, and into social organizations and institutions. Toward the end of the age, the ideas have become fixtures of the civilization, foundational structures upon which the next age will be built. A good analogy is that of a building being built in which each age lays down a row of bricks upon a wall, making the wall one row higher. Each age makes its contribution to the evolutionary process, to be built upon by the succeeding age.

But there is also a downside to this process. There is a kind of 'see-saw' effect; the vitality of the initial ideas diminishes as the outer forms of the society are built. Towards the end of an age the ideas, even while being a great contribution, become crystallized and entrenched. The impulse that formed the age runs down.

There is a metaphor in the East to describe this. The cycle of the ages is called the Wheel of Dharma. The Wheel gets an initiating impulse which spins it every 2160 years. Gradually the wheel runs down. Things get sluggish and stagnant, crystallized and rigid. Then the next zodiacal sign comes in at the beginning of the next age. The Wheel is again spun. There is a new impulse, bringing new ideas and life to initiate new developments in culture and civilization.

We are now in that moment when the Wheel of Dharma is getting its initiating impulse. New ideas and ideals are pouring into the human sphere from the inner planes. New capacities are emerging within the human psyche. New inventions in all walks of life are being discovered.

At the same time, the spinning of the Wheel is happening within the context of the stagnant forms of the Piscean civilization. If we return to the metaphor of spinning a wheel, imagine that the wheel that needs to be spun has become sluggish and encrusted. It is encumbered with crystallized and muddy energies. Thoughts and feelings, social values and mores, institutions and organizations, have become heavy and dense. Though the Piscean energies are withdrawing and diminishing, the crystallized forms or shells of these energies remain large and still possess great momentum. The Wheel that is being spun has to break free of the Old that holds it. The Old that holds it is breaking up and cracking. But as with all things living, the Old holds on to what is known and fights to keep its place.

The Clash between the Old and the New

The beginning of an age is a moment of conflict. The New surges forward with the enthusiasm of youth, as the Old stubbornly resists and fights to keep its dominance. We know this both within our selves and on the larger stage of collective issues. For example, the Aquarian energies that have been coming in since the early 1700s have been stimulating the third eye and activating our intelligence. Although it has had a great influence on scientific thinking and rational thought in the world today, the emotionality of the Piscean period is very much present.

We all have such capabilities of intelligence and understanding, but we can also see the many ways that instinctual emotional-reactiveness still runs us, both individually and collectively, and dominates our thinking patterns. The Aquarian energies have in a brief 100 years changed our civilization into a scientific and information-based society, and awakened in us the next step in the unfoldment of intelligence. Still much of our psychology and many of our organizations and institutions are Piscean.

This struggle between the new life and the crystallized forms is taking place in the subtle sphere of energy which surrounds the planet. You have seen those pictures of the Earth taken from space. Surrounding the Earth is the faint whitish haze of the atmosphere. Imagine that atmosphere not only being composed of air, but also of energy vibrating at the frequency of thought and feeling. Teilhard de Chardin, the French philosopher, called this the noosphere. Others have called it the web. We call it the Matrix. (Not to be confused with the movie 'The

Matrix' though there are some similarities in concept. In the movie, they refer to the matrix as the collective illusion that humanity is dreaming. In some respects, the energy matrix around the Earth is similar in that it contains many collective illusions that keep us in a dream-like state, and from knowing our deeper nature as a soul.)

The Matrix is filled with structures of thought called thought forms. Thought forms can be small, such as when I am carrying the picture of my shopping list for the day. Or they can be large, such as Democracy, or Christianity, or Environmentalism—vast energy structures wrapped into billions of people and thousands of organizations.

When an age begins and the energies of a sign come in, it brings vast and powerful thought forms into the Matrix of energies around the Earth. These large, collective thought forms become the basic foundation of ideas that the civilization is built upon, and they form the underlying structure of ideas and energies upon which almost every single dimension of our lives is built. Just as every moment we are breathing air that gets built into the fabric of our bodies, every moment we are also imbibing thought forms which get built into the fabric of our psyches.

Thought forms continually affect us. They shape our thoughts and behavior. They create specific emotions and determine how we process these emotions. They affect how we handle our instincts and how our super ego is structured. They create the values we hold and the ideals we try to live up to. Thought forms are deeply woven into the inner structure of our psyches and into the outer forms of our institutions.

When a new astrological sign comes in at the beginning of an age, it brings a fundamentally different set of thought forms that conflict with the older established thought forms from the previous age. Let's look at an example of this, one which is affecting all of us today. One of the thought forms from the Piscean Age that is still highly prevalent has been embodied in Christianity and can be stated simply as, "We are born as sinners."

Now compare this thought form to one of the new thought forms of the Aquarian Age that can be stated as, "I love myself, I celebrate myself." This may seem like a minor belief change, but the implications of this 'little' belief shift are radical.

To understand just how profound this attitude is, let's look back for a moment at the effects of the "I am wrong, I should be punished" paradigm. The internal psychological structure of the Piscean human being has become based upon it. This results in guilt, shame, self-denial, and repression. It makes people feel small and weak. They become disempowered, and give their power away to authorities who can dominate them and manipulate them through guilt and fear. People lack confidence with the result that they live small lives, holding to security and avoiding risks because they doubt their capacities to handle what might come up. This feeling bad about themselves makes them overly dependant on the attention and recognition of others. Because they don't recognize themselves, they try in artificial ways to build up a self that others will value. Entire industries—clothing, cosmetics, plastic surgery, television, and many more—are rooted in the psychological compensation mechanisms for these deep self doubts.

Can you imagine a civilization based on the dignity and empowerment of each person? Where people feel deeply woven with the whole, and innately feel valued and that they belong? And where, out of this empowerment, they feel lovingly committed to making the world a better place to live? This type of person enjoys being who they are. They can celebrate their bodies and live richly in their senses, yet be simultaneously connected to their spirituality. They can love themselves and can give themselves permission to be big and bright and beautiful.

The differences in feeling, attitude, and behavior of this type of person are bound to result in significant changes in the social structure. Add up the effects of a few of these 'little' paradigm shifts, and we will ultimately have a very different civilization with a very different inner life for the people in that civilization.

The Struggle of Indigo Souls in a Piscean Civilization

This contradiction between the Old and the New is very challenging, often damaging, to Indigo Souls. A person needs a certain type of nurturance in which to grow—a kind of mental, emotional, and spiritual food. But many Indigo Souls are not getting this. They are not recognized or supported for who they are. The beauty and value of what they carry is not seen. Other people often find them different, perhaps strange. They are sometimes even seen as a threat by those around them. All too often they themselves don't recognize what they carry or who they are. And because they think and feel different and don't fit in, they often judge and negate themselves, sometimes becoming their own worst critics.

We spoke earlier about the situation many Indigo Souls find themselves in: being Indigo Souls in Piscean personalities. This state can be highly problematic for Indigos, because this personality pattern doesn't fit them. It doesn't work well for them. They end up going through life somehow not being themselves. They feel themselves behaving, thinking, and feeling in ways that are not in alignment with who they know themselves really to be deep inside. They may end up doing things, some of which they might even be good at, but which don't nurture their heart or spirit.

In addition, the highly refined sensitivities that are natural to most Indigo Souls are battered and harmed by the denser vibrations of our world today. A common form of this harm is what we call 'the wounding of essence.' To give an example, imagine a highly intelligent Indigo child with an open third eye. Such children have a keen and penetrating insight into things and situations. This child has a lot of clarity as to what is going on within their family. They see the tensions and fears, lies and deceptions, aggressions and competition that are at play, though usually not spoken about.

We all know the innocent directness of children and how they can put their finger on to the heart of an issue, right on to the sensitive places that we adults don't want to talk about. And how do we respond? Often dishonestly; perhaps we say that everything is fine, when really things are not. Or we might more actively shut down the child, telling them to mind their own business, perhaps even punishing them for their intrusion. What do you think this type of behavior does to the child? The capacity of insight that sits in their upper third eye is receiving a hit and it can suffer a wound.

This is just one example of the way a chakra can get wounded. All the chakras can be wounded, and all too often are. In a great number of Indigo Souls the energy field and chakras are contracted and distorted, sometimes even more so than in Piscean Souls who may have suffered similar types of violations.

In addition to this wounding and the feeling of being alien, Indigo Souls need a fundamentally different way of living and relating. But most are not finding it. We all need to make money to pay the bills, but in many cases, the creative spirit in an Indigo Soul cannot earn money with their talents. They may end up working at jobs which are not in resonance with their inner life. It is painful, it is limiting, and it can be destructive to the expansion of life and the flow of energy within them.

The Task of the Indigo Soul Group

All these challenges are part of our task as a soul group. That task is to recognize and externalize the new. It begins by recognizing and honoring the new paradigms, values, and energies that are within us. Then, through inner work, to embody this in our psyches and our lives by becoming fully the people that we know we can be. And lastly, it is to find the courage to express, to build, and to externalize into form the New that we contain.

There is a lot of challenge in this! And there will be a lot of frustration and moments of seeming failure in it. There is not so much support yet, even though things are evolving quickly and great things *are* happening. If we look at the larger picture and see things within a longer span of time, it is all happening very quickly, and positively. The New *is* being born, new vibrations *are* coming in, and a whole new civilization *is* emerging. But if you look at the immediate picture (our particular life, this particular moment in time), many of us are deeply challenged. Many of us are struggling, and in many cases, though we will 'win the war,' we will 'loose many battles' in the process.

It is important that we keep our eyes on the bigger picture and remember that every step we take is another step on the path, and that the path is taking us to great heights, both personally and collectively. It's natural that for ten steps taken we will take a few back. Failures and frustrations are part of the growth and learning process. As individual souls and as a soul group we are journeying through many ages, through many civilizations. In each age we learn different things, have different experiences. We make different experiments and learn from them. Through this never-ending learning process we unfold different aspects of ourselves. What sometimes seems to be a small step in the growth process is a significant contribution to the growth of the whole.

It's also valuable to recognize how important our individual work on our selves is to the whole. Think of each individual as a cell within the body of the planetary organism that we call the Earth. The Earth has a vibratory structure that it has evolved for millions of years. That vibratory structure forms the substance of our bodies, our emotional bodies, our mental bodies, and our energy bodies. As the New is struggling to emerge inside of us, we are working through fears, limiting thought, and emotional patterns that are part of the Earth itself. We are transforming planetary energies when we work on ourselves. We are building a new vibratory structure within our own energy bodies, and our energy bodies are part of the planetary energy body.

As we are making vibratory transformations in what seems to be our personal life, we are making changes to the vibratory substance of the planet itself. So in a sense I am working on the one square meter of the planet that happens to be in the location where 'I' am now standing, just as you are working on your square meter of the planet. And with millions of people working on their square meter, we are changing millions of kilometers. Each one of us is contributing in tremendous ways to the evolving life of the planet, and the emergence of the New. And really, in a very short period of time we are changing thousands of years of vibratory structure.

This moment of the changing of the ages brings the greatest possibility of transformation.

It is very critical for us to do this at this moment. It is in the moment of change as two ages meet, in the chaos of these two conflicting tidal forces, that the New can most easily take shape. There is a very useful metaphor. A man is in a prison; and the prison is well regulated; everything is controlled; everything has its routine; it is very difficult to escape. But if there is an earthquake, and suddenly everything is thrown into chaos, the routines get disrupted and the structures are broken, if a person is alert, he can escape much more easily at that moment.

This is such a moment—there is chaos, there is upheaval in society, there is a breakdown of the old structures before the new structures are built. In this moment, great forces of consciousness are available and are at work. If we can be alert, we can catch this moment. These are the moments when the greatest trans-formations are possible. At a certain point, this moment will have passed. The new Indigo society will have formed and, for all its wondrous next steps, it too will go through the inevitable cycles of development, crystallization, institutional-ization, and decay. The window of the New that we have right now will establish itself into a next step upon the never-ending cycle of the evolution of the ages.

In a way, the next 2000 years hinge upon the depth and richness of the trans-formation that we can bring at this moment of the cusp. We are laying the foun-dations now for the next 2000 years. The more that we can make a positive change now, the more we set a solid foundation for the next age, for the next 2000 years, to be built upon. Great responsibility and great opportunity sits with us.

Questions & Answers

I would now like to open the evening to questions or comments from the group.

I studied business and have been working in these old structures, like banks and corpo-rations. I didn't feel very good there, so I left. I'm now working in a company that does bio-natural products, which suits my nature more but doesn't pay very much money. How can I survive financially in a world that doesn't support these types of things that I enjoy and are good for me?

Finances and business still carry a lot of the old Piscean attitudes where the focus was on productivity, competition, and gain, often at the expense of the employees or the well-being of the individuals. However, the business world is changing rapidly, and there are already many places where business and finance are carrying the New. I foresee in the not too distant future that our workplaces will become significant focal points for our spiritual growth. There is a new spirit in business called 'Consciousness in Business' that is emerging. I see businesses becoming 'corporate ashrams'[1]—businesses or corporations where productivity and inner growth go hand in hand.

Although this new spirit is beginning, we have some time yet to go before it becomes mainstream, and large numbers of people can make their money through working in 'conscious' environments. At the moment, consciousness work will probably not be supported in the normal work environment and most consciously-oriented people probably won't feel at home there.

In a way, you are lucky because you have been able to find a company to work for that carries the New, even though it doesn't pay well. And by working within an alternative-type company, you are in a supportive environment that may help you discover your own unique form of contribution.

There are also other options open to you if you want to make more money. The first is to find a job that works for you within the normal business world but doesn't prostitute you. It might be a more traditional job, but you might be able to find ways to let something of your spirit express through it. You don't change the company or the job, but you find ways of bringing in something of your self.

A second option is that you take the initiative to bring in the New: you begin to make changes to the job, or to the company where you are working. You begin to transform it. You might be surprised at how receptive people are and the many ways in which you can bring in your new ideas.

The third option is to listen inside to what your spirit feels is your calling, and let yourself find a way to create that which you would like to create. Magic happens when you follow your heart and vision. It takes a leap of trust, but I have so often seen that when we jump, life supports us.

One other thing I would like to address. There is a good chance that as a person responding to the New, the people around you may be saying "No, don't do that, go back to the bank, get secure." I want to encourage you to follow your heart and spirit. There are so many voices around us that are based on fear or smallness. They can undermine our vision and our enthusi-

---

1.   The word 'ashram' comes from Sanskrit and refers to a community dedicated to spiritual development.

asm. Trust in yourself. Listen to your inner voice and follow it. As you do, it will make you stronger. Your trust becomes stronger, your flexibility becomes greater, and your ability to adapt to situations becomes more. Trust and courage are muscles that get stronger through being used.

And you will be surprised that you will do your part and existence will do its part. You will survive. You will make the money that you need. It may not be as much as you would like, but it will be enough. I deeply believe that existence finds ways to support us, especially when we follow our calling. And also remember that part of the teaching for many Indigo people is to live simpler, less encumbered by the material. How much do you really need? How much are you getting caught in our culture's preoccupation with having more instead of being more?

Why is this such a special moment? Haven't there been other special moments in history? Do you really feel that this moment is so significant in evolution?

Yes I do. My understanding is that this moment is one of the most significant evolutionary steps that have occurred. This is for two reasons. First, because of the shift between the Piscean and the Aquarian Age. This in itself is highly significant. We are already seeing the changes in society, science, technology, lifestyles, etc. And these are only the tip of the iceberg. I believe that the changes yet to come in the human psyche are even greater.

But there is another reason I feel this moment is highly significant. I believe that at this moment we are preparing for the next step in human evolution. We are in a process of planetary initiation. Planetary initiation is when the planet as a whole makes a quantum jump into the next evolutionary level of consciousness. If you look back in history, there have been some very major moments where evolution has made this type of a jump. One of the greatest of these was when the frontal lobes evolved in monkeys. This was the step that catalyzed the process of monkeys becoming men. I believe that the step that is happening now is as significant, perhaps even more so. It is the step from material man to spiritual man, from instinctual man to conscious man, from man as a physical/psychological entity to man as a vast spiritual entity—the soul.

This is a large and important subject. I will spend more time on it later in these talks.

Shortly before Christmas 2012 is the change in the Mayan calendar. How long will it take for this transformation to take place? Will it be finished at the time the Mayan calendar indicates?

You are asking if I feel this planetary initiation is going to happen by 2012. Well, there are two different voices in me. The first voice says, "I sure hope so! It would be great if we can mature ourselves, and by 2012 humanity makes this great, big jump." I am familiar with the predictions of the Mayans, of Nostradamus and other sources, and they all essentially say that we are going to make an incredible jump sometime in these next 20 years or so. So this is the voice of hope and perhaps wishful thinking in me.

The other voice in me is more pragmatic. It says, "We have a long way to go and a lot of hard work to do. We are in a mess! We can't clean it up so quickly." Perhaps it will take 100 years or 1000 or even 10,000. But in terms of evolutionary time this is quick, it's just the blink of an eye. From our perspective of time, this might seem like a long time, and there is still so much ahead of us. But I deeply believe that it is right now that the process has begun. We are now in the first impulse. I don't know whether the impulse will flower by 2012 or by 20,012, but right now we are setting the stage. Our actions now are critical to the process.

Speaking in a very personal sense, I hope the voice of wishful thinking in me is right, and things really will happen by 2012. But I honestly don't know. The one thing I will say is that the part of me that thinks "It is going to happen by 2012 or 2025" has a lot of what I call the "naïve magical thinking of the inner child." My inner child would like big daddy up there to come along and wave his magical wand and we are all transformed and live happily ever after. But my work as a scientist and psychologist tells me that we have a lot of work to do from our side first. There is no big papa up there who is going to come along and fix everything for us. And at the same time I know that there *is* a magic at play here. There are bigger forces at work than just us.

So, I would say to all of us: let's do our part. It *is* hard work; it is not easy, but clean up your life. And God and the spiritual beings on the other side will do their part. It is a co-creation.

There is something that bothers me about this idea of the Indigo Age or the Aquarian Age. It sounds a bit like it's for the 'chosen few' who are reincarnated under a different sign. But at other times, I understand that the whole of humankind is going to be part of this Indigo Age.

I am reminded of a war movie I saw, 'Private Ryan'. It was D-day and the allies were storming the beaches of Normandy. Soldiers were going against these fortified bunkers and machine guns and being shot down by the thousands. I am not sure that you want to call those that get to charge the bunkers first the 'chosen few', because in some ways that is a bit what it is like. I think it can be quite hard on these early ice-breaker souls. Many progressive souls struggle greatly. But even on a less dramatic level, it can be difficult.

I want to use an example from my own life. My parents are Indigo Souls. Some of the ways it expresses in them is through their progressiveness, open mindedness, humanitarian spirit, and environmental consciousness. They have psychic abilities and are highly sensitive. They were interested in things like Atlantis, psychological development, evolutionary theory, and so much more; and this was in the 1950s and early 1960s before these things became popular.

They were born around the 1930s, at a time where these ideas had little support or understanding. Many qualities of who they were could not flower. My mother wanted to be a geneticist, but ended up becoming a mother and lived in the role of a housewife (even though that role never really suited her nature) because she didn't get support to follow her dreams. At the age of 18, she was already a free spirit who wanted to adventure and travel by herself, but ended up being controlled and channeled into 'acceptable' directions.

My father was turned off to traditional religion but was interested in alternative spirituality. He found no support for these interests and gradually drifted from them, with the result that it kept his spirituality from flowering. He was a scientist who later became the dean of a college. He brought an equalitarian and nonhierarchical spirit to both places, only to be continually hurt, disappointed, and battered by never-ending politicking, back-biting, and competition. His ideas and spirit were way ahead of his time, resulting in pain and frustration for him.

In many ways, both of my parents have been limited and held back due to the times they were brought up in and the effects of those limits upon their inner development. I know that on many levels they don't even know what they missed out on and are okay with the situation, at least on some levels. But I sometimes cry for them for what couldn't flower in their lives.

And with all the limits they had to live with, still they provided a supportive and nurturing environment for my brothers and I to grow up in that allowed more of our spirit to flower. Who can ultimately say about these things, but it is my belief that my parents sacrificed a great deal by coming in early so that they could support us kids.

I'm speaking about them as examples of what it means to be the 'chosen few.' The challenges and difficulties are great. It's not a great ego thing to be one of the 'chosen few,' It's a lot of sacrifice and hard work.

And in response to the bulk of your question, my experience is that there are different groups of souls on the planet at this time, and that many of the souls that are in incarnation now are Piscean Souls who are connected to the past Piscean Age. As they go out of incarnation, most of them will not incarnate again until a much later cycle, many thousands of years down the road. As the Piscean energies withdraw, that soul group goes out of incarnation, and the group of Aquarian Souls start coming in. There are always a few individuals of every soul group, of every sign, in incarnation at any time, but the majority of people in incarnation are of the soul group of the sign that is dominating the times.

And the last thing I would like to say in response to your question is that though the majority of souls in incarnation right now are Piscean Souls, the incoming Indigo/Aquarian energies are affecting everybody. Piscean Souls are also responding, but their response will not be as great as that of the Indigo soul group.

I have done a lot of past life work, and I have the feeling that I have been incarnated quite a few times before. If I am an Indigo Soul, is it possible that I was incarnated during the Piscean Age?

Yes, there is a good possibility that you have had incarnations during the Piscean period. This could be for two reasons. The first is because, as I mentioned a moment ago, there are always some souls from all soul groups in incarnation at any given time. And the second reason is that many Indigo Souls have been preparing to serve in this lifetime through earlier incarnations in the Piscean Age. It is my understanding that some of the early incarnating souls within an age deliberately prepare to do a certain work through several earlier incarnations in the previous age. These incarnations acclimatize them to the age, give them certain understandings, strengths, and skills that allow them to play specific roles or do certain things when the time comes.

This is my own experience. I have many memories of earlier times in which I was trained. When I was 18 years old I 'awoke' in one moment, changing from a rebellious teenager into a seeker and teacher carrying esoteric knowledge that I had brought with me from earlier incarnations. Many Indigo Souls I have met are similar. These incarnations have provided particular training so that you could be of service at this unique juncture in history.

The ages are something new in my knowledge. Is there a historical source of where this knowledge comes from?

There are four sources that I know of that speak about the ages from a spiritual/astrological perspective. The first is from the Hindu traditions, where they are called the Yugas. In India they have a sophisticated calendar system that spans millions of years. There are four main Yugas: Satya, Tretâ, Dvâpara, and Kali.

The second is a stream of wisdom on the planet that is referred to simply as 'The Ageless Wisdom Teachings.' These are believed to be the underlying source of the esoteric teachings throughout all lands in all ages. We inherit remnants of them today, such as the works of Patanjali and the Upanishads from India, Hermetic philosophy from Egypt, the Taoist masters from China, the Zen masters from Japan, and the Sufi masters from the Islamic tradition.

The third body of teaching, one that is more recent, and a source that I believe to be one of the most complete and highest forms of knowledge available today, are the Alice Bailey materials. This body of work is like an encyclopedia of the esoteric, covering a broad range of subjects on evolutionary development and spirituality in an in-depth way.

I would encourage you to read the books from Alice Bailey. They are not easy, but well worth it. In the beginning they are almost impossible to read. You are dealing with, for lack of better words, an 'illumined mind.' The quality of thought and expression is so high, and the thought forms of each sentence are so loaded with information and so vast in their implications, that just the reading of these books begins to open the higher capacities within us. I encourage people who want to accelerate their growth to use these books as muscle building for the soul.

Though all the books are relevant, I think the one that is most immediately relevant to each one of us as a soul on the path of growth is 'A Treatise on White Magic.' White Magic is about the conscious use of energy for inner growth. It teaches us to understand the energies within us. I would also recommend 'Education in the New Age,' as it portrays the growth process of the new souls.

The fourth body of teaching is from the Indian mystic Osho, whom I think of as an Indigo master. His teachings are some of the most modern and progressive. He is a truly rebellious spirit, breaking out from tradition into a free and exuberant state of living.

His teachings address the new spirituality, the new man and woman, and the process of living as a spiritual being in the 21st century. They are life embracing in ways that none of the religions of the past have been. One of the expressions which he is famous for is 'Zorba the Buddha'—a man who can simultaneously live fully in the richness of this world and be fully in the awakened spiritual consciousness of the other world.

What are the signs and the ages? Are they accumulations of souls, or thoughts of God?

In esotericism the 12 Signs of the zodiac are said to be 12 Great Lives, far beyond our evolution, each on its own evolutionary journey. Just like our soul has created the body to experience and learn through, the bodies these Great Lives create are planets and solar systems.

The basis of esotericism is that there is one Great Life that is vast beyond measure, whose body is this Universe. We human beings call that Great Life 'God.' That Great Life steps itself down through a myriad of lesser lives. These lives in turn are stepped down again, and on and on, each lesser in size and caliber and quality. Our lives and even our planet are considered to be relatively far down within this vast hierarchy of lives. Events occurring in the lives higher up from us ripple down and create great currents of energy that move our lives and our world.

Esotericism opens up a very big picture of what life and the Universe are. It gives a sense of an immense oneness of interwoven lives, from the smallest to the Greatest—lives within lives, all interacting and affecting each other in this cosmic scheme.

The ages are thought of as periods within these larger lives. In esotericism there is an expression, "A human lifetime is just a day in the life of the soul."

If this is true, then the soul exists on a much larger scale of time and experience than does our personality.

Now imagine these larger 2160-year cycles created by the zodiacal signs. These are thought of as a day in the life of these great lives. And then there are even larger cycles: the Great Year of the zodiac that encompasses the 12 ages of the signs is 2160 x 12 = 25,920 years. And that cycle is part of an even larger span of time spanning millions of years. So there are many ages, ages within ages, each reflecting the evolutionary process of beings great and small.

3

The Nature of Indigo Souls

As Indigo Souls, you have a fundamentally different inner quality to your think-ing, your feelings, and to the energies that you carry. These differences are a source of much hope and possibilities for the world and for the future, because you carry a sense of values, a vision of potential, a sensitivity and respect for life, and a sense of inter-connectedness that makes your life-affirmative and in honor and support of all living things. As we as a group of souls have more effect upon the world and its structures, we will produce fundamental changes in society.

Freedom

Some of the basic qualities of Indigo Souls are freedom, vision, truth, the need to grow, sensitivity, inclusiveness, holistic perception, and heart-centeredness. Let's explore these, beginning with freedom. Probably one of the most fundamental qualities of Indigo Souls is freedom. You are connected to an inner voice and a rhythm of being. You have a strong sense of yourself and who you are. And because of this it makes it difficult for you to listen to what you are told to do, or 'should' do. You are attuned to this inner life and follow it more easily than you do the outer voices of society or the voices of others around you. Consequently, in many respects you could be called 'Rebellious Spirits.' It is not that you are actively in rebellion for rebellion's sake; it is more that you do not want to follow something that limits life. There is a strong awareness in you if you are being con-trolled, limited, or pressured from the outside. And if you are, you will fight against it.

That fight in you is interesting. It may take the form of outer rebellion or an adamant assertion of 'no.' It often takes a more subtle form—an inner 'no,' even if on the outside you are saying 'yes.' The first type, the obvious 'no' sayers, often get stuck in this rebellion and can spend a lot of energy fighting for their 'rights,' their boundaries, or whatever just cause is in their field of focus. If you fall in this category, your teaching is to learn flexibility, putting yourself to the side sometimes, and learning to compromise in a balanced way. From an energetic level, you need to bring your heart chakra into more activity and relationship with the world around you and 'tone down' your solar plexus. This is not so easy to do because much of your identity comes from 'standing against' something or 'for' something else.

The second type of person, the inner 'no' and outer 'yes' sayer, has a fundamentally different challenge. You are the majority of Indigo Souls. You are basically gentle people. You are not polarized in the solar plexus (the warrior, the fighter, the competitor), which is where the previous soul groups that compose most of humanity today have been focused; you are polarized in the heart. In that sense you are more respectful and gentle; you don't want conflict and you will try to avoid it. This brings one of your fundamental challenges: in avoiding conflict, you often go along with things you don't agree with, or things that you don't feel comfortable with. You compromise. There becomes a division inside of you, a division between what you say and do on the outside, and what you think and feel on the inside, your deeper knowing, your truth sense.

This is one of the areas of challenge for you as an Indigo Soul. The society as it is today is still built on the Piscean Age. One of the downsides of this age is the predominance of masks and roles that hide the inner feelings and the deeper authetncity. And you, like all of us, need to get along with people; you have basic security, love, and communication needs that must be met. The result is that you end up playing roles or wearing masks that are necessary for survival in this society. But these masks never feel right. These roles are too limiting.

Some Indigo Souls can do this and yet, while doing it, can keep in contact with the essential inside. But many of you lose contact with your deeper self. You adapt—but now there is a division—and your Essence retreats. The result is that you live in a kind of an ongoing identity crisis. You may play the role but never quite feel comfortable in it, or you might even function well in the role (because you have a lot of brightness and creativity that comes through it), but somehow you are not really nurtured by it.

Many of you will take on the role because it is necessary, but underneath your rebellious spirit fights against the falseness and restrictiveness of it and may sabotage it. This is a big theme for many Indigo Souls: how are you sabotaging the roles or situations that you are in?

Because of all these dynamics with false roles, masks, and identity, many Indigo Souls are struggling with their identity in the society, with success, and with outer accomplishments. Either you can't play the role, or you can't find a role that you are willing to play, or you are playing the role but are fighting and sabotaging it.

So one of the major teachings for Indigo Souls is the right meaning of freedom and individuality. There are different levels:

There is freedom-against or rebellion-against. For example, I might be against repressive society, or I might be against authoritative control. That is the first level.

The next level is different: instead of freedom 'against,', it is freedom 'for.' It has to do with, "What do you value?" Instead of being against something, you are seeking to create something new that is of value to you. You are living for your vision.

Ultimately, there is an even higher level of freedom—the freedom to be your real self. It is the freedom from the limiting aspects of your personality structure. Then, no matter the limitations of the outside world, which will always be limited, you are free in your consciousness.

Indigo Souls are Visionaries

Vision is one of the deepest notes reverberating in the Indigo Souls. You have a deep sense of carrying something 'new,' carrying something that you feel is a 'better' way, a more life-affirmative way. You aspire toward a higher possibility. You have probably been seeing possibilities since you were very young.

Perhaps as a child you were always asking, "Why should we do it this way; it seems limiting; it seems disrespectful, why? I know there is a better way." You have sensed that there is a better way. And there *is* a better way! You may not have been supported when you talked of it. You may have felt like a lone voice crying in the darkness, so you may have learned not to trust your insights, but no matter how much you distrusted or fought against them, they didn't go away. This is the spirit of the new that is calling you.

Sometimes we don't see the new, we just feel frustrated with the old. We don't know what the new is, we just feel locked in, restless, dissatisfied. You look at society, its institutions, organizations, and forms of relating, and are keenly aware of the limits and the restrictiveness of these forms. It is good that you see this because it keeps you from getting caught and ensnared in these collective forms. But this can also be destructive to you. Your mind can get caught in a negative loop. Then you see what's wrong but you don't look to see what can be made right. You focus on the problem instead of seeing the solution.

If that is the case for you, then I invite you to look deeper. Your dissatisfaction is because something of the spirit is imprisoned and not flowing. You sense there can be something better, freer, more liberated, more life supportive. Your challenge is to look for the new possibilities and what is a next better step: to find your vision and then to act and to become creative, to become communicative and expressive of your vision.

This is very challenging. It is one of the greatest challenges to follow your heart, your vision and spirit, especially in the face of non-understanding from others or outright adversity. In so many ways, when you come forward with your vision you get cut down. You may be told things like, "stop dreaming," "get real," "get your feet on the ground," "come live in the real world," "stop being naïve,"…So many negative messages are communicated to you verbally or non-verbally. Occasionally you get support and find resonance, but to a great extent you don't.

Remember, that you are here as an agent of change. You are here to begin to live and embody—in your own life, in your own way of Being—something new. And you are here to express that to others in a respectful way. It takes courage.

Bright souls, visionary souls have always been coming into incarnation. These are the souls who were burnt at the stake, who were persecuted by the Inquisitions. So in the collective racial memory, there is a deep fear of the new vision that you carry inside of you. This fear of persecution sits deep in your cells. In many ways this is one of the greatest fears that you need to overcome. Your vision and your truth have been life threatening in the past and your protection system is deeply threatened by them.

And yet, we probably live now, at least in the Western part of the world, in the most open and liberal society that may ever have existed. A wise woman in the past that worked with herbs, energy, and healing would have been called a witch and burned; now she puts up a poster in a health food store and has a Web site. It is a different age, a different time. There is a freedom and a permissiveness today that is wonderful. So the limits and fears that we have are based on racial memory more than on reality now. That doesn't deny that in some ways you are still a misfit and a stranger to many people around you. Although it might and probably will lead to a certain amount of rejection, non-understanding, ridicule, or separation, it's not life threatening. You can handle it.

And more than handle it; it is your challenge and your responsibility to become the builder of your vision. First, above all else is to honor the seeds of the new that you see inside. You carry many, many pictures and images of new ways of being. It is as if your soul has a blueprint of the full flowering of possibilities that are seeking to unfold at this time within human beings. You have a sense of a new way of being psychologically and spiritually healthy, a new way of relating with the body, with nature, with material objects. You see new forms of relationships; new forms of communication; new forms of work, career, and making money; new understandings of power; new forms of society. You have ideals of a new medicine, a new education, a new form of family, government, etc. And I want to say to you clearly: you are not a dreamer with your head in the sky. What you carry is a recognition of something that is held in the inner world as a blueprint of a whole new way of living and of being.

It is as if you are a seed that has written into your genetic blueprint what kind of a flower or tree you should become. Your sense of this blueprint is very real in your inner consciousness. In some ways, it is probably one of the strongest and most powerful forces in your life. Just to exemplify this: try to imagine giving up your dreams and living a traditional, conservative life without any higher meaning or purpose. You cannot!

That is the force of the new, that is the force of the vision calling you. You are a visionary. Listen to your vision and trust it. Give it space in your feelings and thoughts; give it space in your actions, relationships and in what you say. Through doing so you are evolving the world! You are building new thought forms into the dimension of thought that surrounds the planet. You are creating new emotional and energetic vibrations and structures within the energy world that surrounds the planet. Recognize your potency as a builder. You, together with many others, are building new frequencies, new paradigms, and inner energy states, and later those energies will take outer forms and structures.

The Intuitive Sense of Truth

One of the other areas that is of prime importance to you is what I would call an 'intuitive sense of truth.' You have a sense of what the inner core of things is. For example, a person may be saying "Hello," and smiling and behaving nicely, but you may sense that that person is putting on a mask and is in pain inside. You may see that a person is behaving generously, but sense that underneath the person is being manipulative or tricky. This 'truth sense' runs deep in you. You have 'a love of truth.' When truth is there it has a kind of clean and pure sound that you feel in your body, and that makes your spirit rejoice.

The challenge that you face is that we live in a world of deceptions and lies. We live in a society that is based on appearances, not on truth. We are brought up as children to behave in a certain way, to show a certain face. The result is that many of us have to repress our truth sense. We have to repress our own feelings.

Maybe we feel uncomfortable about something that is happening, but to handle the situation without extra friction we have to smile and make-nice about it.

One of the greatest losses that happen to us is that many of us disconnect, at least on the conscious level, from our truth sense. Perhaps we get caught in the way we think we should behave, or in the way we have been taught to behave. Or perhaps we put on blinders. We may see the good in other people but our filters are blocking us from seeing the destructive patterns that person is carrying, with the result that we get hurt.

We do not want to see things that are not so comfortable. And that is our challenge: to see that there is both light and dark. Human beings carry within them a broad spectrum of energies, ranging from some very bright and wonderful spiritual dimensions to some very dark, dense, and frightening energies. Most of us have learned to not see the darkness. But it is there. It is operative and having its effects. So an important part of your challenge is to have the courage to open your eye, your 'third eye,' to see the truth of what is. And that means in your self as well.

We don't want to see the darkness in our self. Many of us are also afraid to see the light in our selves because it means we might stand out. We are afraid to acknowledge our intelligence, our strength, our vision, our love, and our spirituality.

Seeing the truth is wonderfully refreshing. If you see a problem and you look it in the eye, then you know what the problem is and you can do something about it. If you deny a problem and make-nice and gloss over it, all you have done is to push it under the carpet where it festers and creates more problems.

The same is true on the opposite side. If you are dealing with truth, you are dealing with what is real in the depths of yourself and the other person. In a sense 'truth equals intimacy,' because if you are in your truth, and the other is in their truth, then there is a meeting of the inner with the inner, instead of a meeting of the mask that veils with the mask of the other that veils, as is normally the case. How can intimacy happen between masks? It is like two knights in medieval armor trying to hug each other. How intimate can you get when you are behind a wall of armor and protection?

So, as Indigo Souls you are entering a new dimension of relating: a dimension based on honesty, on real communication, on the intimacy that comes through real communication. And to become real means to put your walls and your masks away and let your self be seen and become more vulnerable. So truth, honesty, intimacy, and vulnerability are all deeply woven together. You are seeking this form of relating, and nothing else will satisfy you.

The Deep Longing of Indigo Souls to Grow

Your truth sense is connected to one of the deepest needs and longings of all Indigo Souls, your desire and calling to grow. You are blessed and cursed with a perpetual sense of dissatisfaction: with who you are, with what the world is. One part of you is always, always aware that you could be more—more loving, more in your energy, more sensitive, more powerful, more, more, more—in a thousand different ways more. And that is true. Your soul is calling you to be more. Your soul is stretching you to be more. In so many ways you are constantly working on yourself, challenging yourself, pushing yourself to be more.

I describe it as a blessing and a curse because on one hand, the blessing is that through this stretching you *are* becoming more. In the process you are giving birth to yourself, giving birth to a whole new way of being, giving birth to a new humanity. So your calling and your urge to grow is, in many ways, the greatest contribution you can make to the building of the New Humanity.

But the curse is that you are so often not satisfied with yourself. There are two wonderful inner sub-personalities, The Critic and The Perfectionist that get in gear and beat you up for not being perfect. And they pull in a third sub-personality called The Pusher that then drives you remorselessly to be more. In the old society, the force of the Pusher was focused on achievement in the world, on having outer success. For Indigo Souls the Pusher is about becoming spiritually more. You may not care so much about having great outer success and millions of dollars (Of course you wouldn't mind it if you had it! And for many of us, our inner growth is intimately woven with outer success.), but instead you care about greater authenticity, having a more open heart, being more in your energy, being more in truth, being more connected, and on and on.

So your task is to learn the wonderful art of what they call in Zen, 'Wu Wei': the art of doing without doing; working without working; being totally in your energy, and totally relaxed. That means trying to build a new world and seeing a future that is wonderful, and giving it your 100 percent energy to create it, and at the same time not being attached and being in acceptance of what is right now. We are learning to accept and enjoy what is with all its limits and imperfections even while working to change it.

Questions & Answers

I would now like to open the talk up for questions and participation.

• *I am carrying this fear of ending like John F. Kennedy, and I wonder if this is just my fear, or is it a kind of collective fear that I am feeling?*

> Our collective unconscious holds a deep fear of persecution: it is not safe to be too creative, too bright, too much in your truth. Look at our history and what has happened to so many great people who have been speaking their truth—Jesus, Socrates, Mahatma Gandhi, Martin Luther King, and so many others. Your fear is very realistic.
>
> Though we still have reasons today to be fearful, things are so much better than they have ever been. So these fears are not so much in response to the realities of today, they are more shadows from our past. They are passed on through the collective unconscious, and possibly through the genes, or through memories of past lives. These fears also result from innate fears from our instincts of being different than our peer group with the resultant judgments.
>
> What I'm seeing for you personally is that you are not energetically fully present. It's as if you are floating above yourself and your feet are not planted firmly on the ground. This can be the result of deep persecution fears. When we have such a fear we don't want to bring our selves fully into the body. I also see that you are a passionate person and the calling to speak and live your truth is strong. And that the fear of persecution is inhibiting you to act and live and fully be here. It is a big step to work through these fears and to make the decision to come into the body and to really live here.

• *I am afraid of stepping into personal responsibility and power, like I will make mistakes if I come into my power.*

> A soul can incarnate with a sense of mission and purpose to contribute and help change things—to be an agent of change in a society in transition. My sense for you is that this is not the first time that you have done this in a moment of collective change. Those earlier times were much denser. The human vehicle was not as evolved as it is now. The instinctual forces were rawer. Consequently, many very bright souls who came into denser and rougher vehicles got caught and used their power and aggression and intelligence in ways that were not so refined or loving or harmonious. Almost every light worker that has existed on this planet has misused power; and has suffered through it. The forces that were so raw and powerful in you would take over, even while other parts of your consciousness suffered because of it.

I think part of our lesson as light workers is to learn acceptance, forgiving-ness, and compassion for our imperfections as light workers, and then to have the courage to jump in again, willing to do our best, knowing we are going to make mistakes. You are in good company; there are only imperfect light workers on the planet. Let me make it very clear: as Indigo Souls enter-ing this New Age, we have more power available to us internally because of our consciousness and because of our technologies and the growth of knowl-edge than we have ever had before. Many of us would like to think of the New Age as an age of love, light, and celebration. But I would like to say that in addition, it is an age of power. It is our task to use that power—creatively, with love and intelligence, and not to shy away from it. We are powerful people and as we evolve we are only becoming more powerful. I see spiritual growth as a growth into handling greater levels of energy and power, and learning to handle them with greater love and intelligence.

• *I have the feeling that even today a lot of light workers misuse their power. Although it is meant well, they still misuse it. I would like to see us look at this and deal with it in a more honest way.*

We as human beings have never really addressed the issue of power honestly. If you look at our political situation in the world today, it is essentially an alpha male power game of who rises to the top. Even in our so-called enlightened and modern age, how many politicians are out there that we can say we truly respect and honor? The forces of ego, domination, and power still wrap human beings deeply. And the exact same forces that we see in the political world are operating in the spiritual world: ego, competition, domi-nation, comparison, etc. You look at the church and you see constant power struggles throughout its history.

And why should we, just because we are in a New Age and carry some new energies, think that we are beyond all that? We are not. The New Age and the light workers in the world, all of us have a lot to learn about power. And that will be one of our challenges as we move into deeper levels of honesty and truth: to start looking at our power issues and working on them.

• *You talk about truth, but it is not actually graspable for me. What is truth?*

Let's say that truth, at this moment and time, would be a sense inside of you as to what you really feel or really see in a situation. Not that it is the Ulti-mate Truth, or that it is even right. We call it, 'Listening In.' Somehow it is as if you turn your ear inwards and you hear what your inner is saying or feeling. And what you start to recognize is that we have many levels of response and feeling. For example, someone says to you, "Would you like to do this?" Part of you will feel, "Oh yes that is fine." But as you look deeper you notice that there is a little something uncomfortable in your belly and as you start to penetrate more you find that you are not so fine with that. You didn't want to say it, perhaps because it would embarrass you, or hurt them, or something. So by listening in you penetrate through the surface layers and begin to feel deeper feelings and perceptions that you have and might not have been so comfortable with.

And then there is a way of communicating from this perception of truth. Instead of saying, "The truth is…(which tends to sound like the Ultimate Truth given by God Almighty)," you're saying, "My truth, as much as I know it in this moment is…"

I can ask in any situation, "God direct me to the truth," and I always get a clear answer.

It is beautiful that you have such a direct connection to the Transcendent, and that answers come so clearly. It is something to treasure and that you can rely upon. At the same time, I want to give you a word of caution. I would be very careful of believing that everything you hear is God speaking directly to you. As you sit with that 'truth' and go deeper into it, it may change and evolve. It is the nature of the mind to want to have absolutes, and there is nothing more absolute than the feeling that, "God told this and this is THE truth and that's the way it is." It is easy to fool our self, easy to hypnotize our self. And with you in particular, one of the dangers that I would alert you to is the hypnosis of believing that, "What I have just heard is God, or my higher self, my guides, or some inner authority figure speaking the absolute and ultimate truth." Perhaps it is. Treasure the insights and what you hear. And at the same time be alert, be discriminative.

• *I am having a big struggle with speaking my truth. I sense that I have so much in me to contribute and bring out, that I have talents, that I am really good at some things, but I am really in a struggle to own it and express it.*

I see two things. First that there is a fear in you to come out, and stand out, because the moment you stand out is the moment you can be pulled down. It is almost a genetic fear in our cells: "Don't stand out too much," "Don't be different," "Don't be too visible," "Definitely don't be better," because it is dangerous. And the second fear results from a set of cultural beliefs: that we are sinners, we are wrong, don't be egotistical, be humble. As if it is a sin in God's eyes to say, "I am great." There is a fear that if I did that, I will be punished. So it takes a lot of courage with both those fears to step out and let your self shine.

Yes, and at the same time there is such a big drive in me, sometimes I can't contain it, it is so present and it is so strong to go and to do, and just to be doing what I am here to do. Sometimes I feel, "Why is this old stuff holding me back?" It is not going fast enough for me, I want to drop this old coat, it is clinging to me too much.

When I was 19 years old, I was studying therapy in Arizona with a man who was about 50. He was a highly respected group leader, therapist, and spiritual leader in the community. One night we were talking in a restaurant. During the conversation he said in a very matter-of-fact kind of way in response to something we were speaking about, "I am a top therapist." I remember my reaction: I kind of jerked back in my seat and thought, "Oh, what an ego trip." And then I looked at my reaction, and I realized that he *was* a top therapist, he was a superb therapist and recognized as such in the community, and he had said it not as a puffing of his ego, but just in a very matter-of-fact way in the course of the conversation. I realized that basically he had just said the truth, and he was comfortable with it. It was the first time I had ever seen someone who so clearly knew themselves, honored themselves, and could just let themselves be what they are. He set an example for me to live up to.

• *I see in my kids how normal it is for them to be in their truth, and it makes me humble about how can I educate them and raise them up. Somehow all I can do is give them love and allow them to grow—they already seem to know so many things much better. I think the teachers are afraid of them. They have 30 individuals like them in the class and they are telling the teacher the truth, "Look at what you are doing," and the teachers are getting very frightened. It is hard for teachers to find their way.*

I have a feeling that kids start life by knowing the truth, and it is we parents who condition them out of it. I know you as a parent: you have a lot of listening space for your children's essence and truth, and a lot of respect to not limit them, or impose your system of beliefs on them. That doesn't mean that you are perfect, or that you haven't done your part to condition them. But when you have done things, you quickly notice and try to rectify them.

One of the reasons for this is that you are an Indigo Adult who has Indigo kids. Your kids are lucky because they are getting a nurturing environment where they are fundamentally understood and supported. I am reminded of Kahlil Gibran's book 'The Prophet' where he talks about children. He says, "Your children are not your children. They are the sons and daughters of Life's longing for itself. They come through you but not from you, and though they are with you, yet they belong not to you. You may give them your love but not your thoughts. For they have their own thoughts. You may house their bodies but not their souls, for their souls dwell in the house of tomorrow, which you cannot visit, not even in your dreams. You may strive to be like them, but seek not to make them like you."

To live what he is speaking about takes quite a mature state in a parent or a teacher. To let the children be, to be available to give them what they need; to avoid the tendency to want to package them and to let them find their own.

When you spoke about school, it reminded me of something. I can't remember the exact numbers, but there is something like 8 million children in Germany who are on the drug Ritalin as a way to counter what is seen as attention deficit disorder. A lot of these very bright and energetic kids are not wellbehaved. They are in touch with themselves and a deeper truth sense and way of being, and are following it. But the teaching model in the schools is still in the old way. These kids overwhelm and frighten their teachers. The teachers react by trying to close the kids down, put them in a box, or drug them. So there is a great challenge that the school systems face: instead of trying to make the children fit into the school, the school has to transform to fit these new children. The schools need to develop a new education for these new souls.

4

Sensitivity, Holistic Thought, Heartfulness, and the New Spirituality

Heightened Emotional and Energetic Sensitivity

In the last section, we began looking at some of the primary qualities of Indigo Souls, and we covered freedom, vision, truth, and the need to grow. Let's continue by looking at one of the primary qualities that Indigo Souls carry: that of heightened sensitivity. What this means is you feel deeper on both an emotional and an energetic level. You sense the emotional currents and moods in yourself or in other people. And on an energetic level you can sense the subtle vibrations of a person, or a location. You can sense the vibrations from nature, machines, animals, etc. You can sense beneath surface appearances to the 'nuances' that are happening—if a person is sad or happy or collapsed, things like that. This gift allows you a deeper level of intimacy with life because it allows you to be more fine-tuned in relating.

At the same time it brings you certain challenges. The majority of people are not aware of the energetic dimension of themselves. For example, something happens in an interaction and a person gets emotionally hurt. You ask them if they are okay, and they say that they are fine and nothing is wrong. But you can sense that they are hurt, that they are collapsed, that they are defensive, that something has shifted in them. You pick up these energetic subtleties quite accurately. However, most people don't register them so clearly, and are often in denial of them.

It is often strange for you in communicating or interacting, because you want to relate to the truth of what is there, but the normal level of communication is based on the roles and masks that hide rather than reveal the truth. The result is that many Indigo Souls learn to distrust themselves. Instead of saying, "Well, I am seeing that this person is hurt, even if they are denying it," you say to yourself,

39

"Well, I must be imagining things, maybe I am just making it up." You may not trust yourself and your perceptions. This makes you a little bit insecure. Your gut-level response is to the truth of what is there, but the situation makes you respond to the surface. And that is an untruth, it is a role, it is not solid.

So you are often a little insecure in life, and you think there is something wrong with you. Actually there is something very right about you, but it hasn't been supported. In a sense it is a central teaching for you to learn to trust your perceptions. That is not easy to do. The world of energy is vast and subtle and full of different types of forces at work, much more than we normally talk about. To give you an example, the Eskimo people in Alaska have something like 26 different words for the word snow: there is dry snow, wet snow, heavy snow, light snow…Their language has developed many nuances to describe snow.

The languages that we speak don't yet have the nuances of energy. Let's look at the use of the word 'love.' When someone says, "I love you," that word can have so many subtleties to it. Someone says they love you, and it is the paternal type of protective love. Or in another moment they might love you, but there is a neediness pulling on you. Or someone says, "I love my new car." There are so many subtleties of love. We are often not attuned to these nuances, nor can we verbalize what we perceive. So our challenge is to trust our sensitivity, to trust ourselves, and to learn to cognize. Cognize means to let these subtle feelings move into our mind, our consciousness, up here in the third eye, that we can then say, "It is this or that specific quality."

The opening of this sensitivity corresponds with a development in the upper petal of the third eye. We spoke earlier about the two components of the third eye: the lower and the upper. The lower component is the analytical, rational mind. The upper component is the intuitive mind. It has insights into things; it senses the flow of different sorts of energies. It is through the upper petal of the third eye that we sense there is an inner world behind the outer world that we know.

I want to elaborate for a moment on a theme I spoke of earlier regarding this: the capacity of self-reflection. One of the major developmental tasks for humanity today is to open more fully the upper third eye, and in particular, the ability to look more deeply into our selves. Normally if you ask someone, "How are you feeling?" they might say, "I feel fine," and that is really what they would have perceived. Yet as an outsider you could see that there was a lot more going on. They didn't have the capacity to turn inwards and look more deeply at themselves.

This capacity of self-reflection, self-awareness, is unfolding rapidly now for great numbers of people as the Indigo/Aquarian energies come in. It is bringing us a whole new set of challenges that will require training and understanding to be handled rightly. One of these is that, as the third eye opens you become aware of an almost overwhelming amount and variety of energies. Many people are suffering from what could be called an overload of energetic and emotional impressions. You are picking up so much that you can't handle it. For example, you might be with a group of people and begin to feel overwhelmed, confused, or exhausted. This can be due to the many energies that are at play. An important aspect of what could be called 'self-awareness training' is the ability to understand the many forces that work within and around you, and to be able to clearly differentiate between the many different types of energies that are at play. At the more advanced levels of this type of training you learn to consciously handle and control these energies.

Holistic Thought

Another quality that opens with the upper third eye is a different type of thinking. For lack of better words, we can call it 'holistic thought.' Holistic thought perceives the interrelation of things and how they affect each other. A good example of holistic thought in the world today is the Green Movement. The Green Movement is an awareness of how human life is interdependent on plant life, on the atmosphere, on the ocean—how all of these things are related and connected together.

We see the opposite of holistic thought in the self-centered developers who are destroying the rain forests for short-term profit and personal gain. Of course, there are always exceptions to this in specific situations, but in general these people's view is myopic. They see only what is in front of them and are not aware of the larger implications. They are blind to the bigger picture. It's not that these people are selfish or greedy (certainly many of them are), but there is another factor at play. In them, the third eye is closed or has blinders in front of it. They don't yet have the capacity to see a bigger picture.

Great numbers of people now are undergoing an opening of the third eye and are beginning to see the larger interrelatedness of things. They are seeing the interconnectedness: how 'I' am affected by things from many directions and how 'I' affect things in many directions. This creates an expansion of identity. For example, I begin to think, "I am a part of the Earth and the life of the Earth. It is not so clear that I am a separate entity here because I am so interrelated with the life of the Earth. Where do I stop, and where does the Earth begin?"

This type of thought is changing many things in the world, because once you start to see this way you cannot just sit back while things are happening elsewhere that are doing damage to the planet. If people are starving in Africa, you may not be directly faced with it here in USA or Europe, and yet it is affecting us. It affects the emotional tenor of the world atmosphere. This kind of awareness makes us care for the planet and other people in a wider way than we ever have before. I would venture to say that one of the greatest contributions of Indigo consciousness is the recognition of the planet as a living, interrelated system.

If you think about it, it is only in the last 50 years, or even less, that there has been this expansion of interrelated consciousness on the planet as a whole. If you think of one or two hundred years before, nations existed pretty much within an isolated bubble of their own. There were only a few small links, via a road or a shipping lane, to another nation and the amount of exchange was minimal. If you look at the last 150 years (I am not sure exactly if it is 150 or 200 years), first we had railroad lines, then cars leading to a vast road system. We had the development of steam ships that moved quickly across the oceans, air transport across the planet, telegraph, telephone, radio, television, and now the satellite and data communication networks.

In a very short period of time, we have built on the planet these many forms of interrelatedness that have never existed. These outer forms correspond with an opening of consciousness inside of us. We are thinking more globally, we are thinking on a planetary level, we are aware of interrelatedness, and we are aware of things that are affecting us and that we are affecting in many directions.

This holistic sense is going to develop even more. There are parts of us that are still very personal in our thinking: "This is my life, my problems, my issues." Gradually you begin to recognize that what is happening in you is a reflection of things that are happening all over. For example, great numbers of people have difficulties these days in relationships because the old forms of male/female roles are changing. But most of us don't yet see that the problem that "I have with you in our relationship," is part of a global shift in consciousness. The energy centers in people are shifting as part of a collective movement in consciousness, and it is changing their personalities, identities, roles, relationships, etc. The ways that we used to relate have to change. The ways that we define our individuality in relationships is changing. The ways that we are being challenged to communicate is changing.

Our so-called 'problem' is part of a vast movement of evolutionary energies that are changing in millions and millions of people; just as in a bath tub if you were to start moving your hand back and forth, the water starts sloshing back and forth. If you could imagine the planet from above, as an energetic force, there are energy waves that are moving on the planet from this direction to that direction.

These waves are composed of energetic, mental, and emotional substance. This is what holistic perception brings you: you begin to see the planet as this vast, pulsating, moving system of emotion, thought, and energy patterns. And as you see that you realize that it is affecting you, tremendously so.

This recognition goes in two directions. As you recognize your interrelationship with the whole and the effects it has upon you, you also recognize that you have much more effect on the whole than you ever perhaps realized. Because changes that happen in you ripple outwards. The more potency you hold, the more your energy makes ripples. One of the repercussions of this awakening of holistic perception is the empowerment of the individual.

Holistic Thought and the Heart Center

The opening of holistic thought occurs not just within the third eye, but also within the heart center. Heart consciousness, the state of consciousness opening through the heart center, holds a deep respect for life. For example, if someone said to you, "Go over and harm that plant," you could not do it. It hurts you, because a part of you feels how you are connected to the plant and how your life and its life are related. It is like doing harm to yourself. These feelings come about through the opening of the heart center. There have been many cultures which have been holding heart-consciousness, especially some of the indigenous peoples, and certainly many individuals in all cultures. But by and large, for the greater mass of humanity the aspects of the heart that are related to a bigger picture have been relatively closed and dormant. The third chakra or solar plexus, the center beneath the heart, was more active.

The lower part of the third chakra is concerned with power, action, aggression, selfishness, and ego. In third chakra consciousness, personal gain is what's important; the welfare of others is important only because it supports you. Seen in an evolutionary perspective, this third chakra phase of evolution was a necessary developmental step. But we are passing out of that phase now. The valuing of other living things is a reflection of a rapidly growing heart consciousness. When we are in heart consciousness we cannot harm other people, we cannot harm animals or plants. There is an attunedness and a resonance—their pain is our pain. This is why the heart chakra is called the unity chakra. Through the heart there is a fundamental oneness, a unity. We are no more separate.

This sense of honoring and valuing life at a collective level is still relatively new. It is the nature of evolution that as new faculties open, they are not yet balanced within the overall psyche. Because of this, the opening of the heart center is bringing certain challenges and difficulties to us. Many Indigo Souls have polarized in the heart center but in the process have 'turned off', so to speak, the solar plexus. What that means is that you have become gentle, but you have lost the potency of your power. You may get more easily run over by the power of other people. Or you may give your power away too easily. Or it may not be so easy for you to stand for what you want.

A second issue is that power sometimes needs to be destructive for something constructive to emerge. So an important teaching for many Indigo Souls is to integrate power with your heart: to become a loving person and a powerful person, to be gentle and to be strong.

In growth work we use three words in a special way: sympathy, empathy, and compassion. Let's use an example to clarify. Imagine a person who gets hurt because he or she is in a pattern of dependency. They are extremely needy for the attention of another and energetically pull on them. The other, feeling suffocated, pushes them away. This person then feels rejected and blames the other for not loving them.

A sympathetic response to this person's pain would be to feel sorry, or even pity, for them. Sympathy might say: "You poor baby, how terrible that he abandoned you."

Empathy means, if you are in pain, I feel your pain, I am in resonance with your pain. I don't just feel sorry for you from a distance, I feel with you. Empathy might say: "I know that hurts. I feel with you."

Compassion brings a level of understanding and clarity in addition to the empathy. Compassion might say: "I feel your pain and I know you're hurting. This isn't easy for me to say, and might not be easy for you to hear, but I see you repeatedly tripping over this same thing again and again. You give your self away to people, expect them to be the all and everything for you, and then you feel rejected when they aren't. My sense is that until you face this issue you are going to stay in the same pattern and repeatedly get hurt."

Compassion brings love and understanding to the underlying problem. It helps people face their issues and grow. Compassion deals with truth. It may create more pain for them at that moment, because it is painful to look at our patterns. But it is only by looking at them that the patterns can be changed and things can be shifted. Compassion sometimes requires us to create pain in the process of creating wholeness.

We have to take a risk that our words might hurt the other. But truth, spoken with love, creates the hurt that heals. It is the hurt that comes because we have revealed a wound that has been hidden. It is the hurt that comes because a mask or a role that is not of our Essence is being torn up. And think about this: to leave a person in those bubbles, behind those walls, will hurt them more in the long run, because you cannot grow when you are hidden behind roles and masks and walls. This person may spend a great portion of his or her life in the same repeating pattern and pain. There is a beautiful saying by Buddha about this: "A lie is sweet in the beginning but bitter in the end. Truth is bitter in the beginning but sweet in the end."

So when I say you are learning to integrate power with your heart, you are learning to use the solar plexus power in a way that is direct with people, go for things, stand for your self, and yet is loving and supportive and gentle in the process.

To put this in a larger perspective, humanity was polarized in third chakra power for a long period of time. The energies are now swinging to the opposite pole of heart-centered gentleness. And this is very much needed. You carry that gentleness well in you, but you are not in balance; you often do not have the potency that you need for successful living. You need to be more direct, sometimes more confrontative. You need to speak more from your truth and stand up for what you think and see. You need to have the courage to go for things that you want and believe in. You have repolarized into the heart and that is beautiful, but you have lost some of the qualities of strength that the power center brings you. The third and fourth chakras need to integrate. The humanitarian values and the sensitivity that are opening need to be integrated with your power. Together they create dynamic potent living and action in which your values have an effect on life.

Indigo Souls Have Strong Spiritual Longings

This opening of the heart in connection with the crown chakra is affecting the spiritual dimension in you. You sense a spiritual possibility in life. You have a spiritual longing. At the same time your rebellious Indigo nature does not want to be controlled, put in a box, or be told how to think. That part of you rebels against the traditional religious frameworks. You are familiar with the saying, "Don't throw the baby out with the bath water." Many of us, in our rebellion against limiting religious structures, have also thrown out our spirituality. The ownership of your spiritual nature is essential and an important part of your process of self-development. Your spiritual longing is tremendous and it is essential for you to find ways to follow it.

In a certain way, spirituality for you is something that will be a very personal journey. It is a looking inwards, a listening inwards. It is an experimentation with your self. You are learning to open the doors of spirituality through self-exploration and self-development, rather than following a prescribed path. The spirituality of the past was emotional and rule based. In many ways it required you to put aside your intelligence: you were taught to believe, not to question; you were taught to follow rather than find your own way. But we are no more followers. We do not want to believe something because someone tells us to; we want to understand, we want to think about it, we want information, and we want to make our own decisions. This is a great step—we are becoming intelligent people, we are becoming mature.

And again, evolution is rarely in balance. In this process we have become overly mental. Many of us have dismissed the emotional, feeling, mystical, and devotional side of our selves. In a way our thinking has become rational, mental, scientific, critical, but we have lost touch with the mystic and the ecstasy seeker, with the Zorba and with our passion. We are now learning to find a form of spirituality that encompasses the opposites of feeling and intelligence, intuition and intellect, logic and mysticism, the transcendental and the worldly.

We are learning a whole new form of spirituality. In a sense we have to pioneer it. We are new human beings with new capacities opening in our energy systems, with new parts of the brain and psyche awakening, new emotions, new thoughts, new ways our energies are flowing. Our approach to inner development and spirituality needs to reflect the changes that are happening in us. Our spirituality is a deeply powerful longing. We must understand it, live it, and give it form so that it can flower. This type of spirituality needs to encompass the emerging qualities of sensitivity, holistic thought, interconnectedness, and loving power. This will create a new approach to the spirit, a new spirituality.

Questions & Answers

• *Kabir, I see from what you spoke about earlier my neediness and how I act on it, and the pains that I have from this neediness. How do I manage it, how do I deal with this neediness? The longing to have a woman is very natural, so does this mean that I should just let go of this longing?*

The problem is that your heart *is* opening, but as your heart opens your belly center, which is connected with the heart center, also opens. The belly is where our emotional needs for closeness, belonging, and security are. These needs are natural, normal, and must be met. Unfortunately, as most of us didn't have the ideal childhoods, we have many unfulfilled needs sitting in our bellies that go all the way back to our childhood. These unfulfilled needs are part of a complex called the wounded inner child. What happens is that now, as an adult, when your heart connects with a woman your belly also becomes active and the wounded inner child with its unfulfilled needs arises. Instead of being an adult with your heart open to a woman, you become a needy child with a woman. This causes several levels of pain: the pain from the unfulfilled needs, the pain that's been sitting from the past, and the pain arising from the adult part of you that is observing your neediness. You lose respect for yourself and feel ashamed.

The issue that so many of us men are faced with is, how can we as men handle our unfulfilled emotional needs from childhood? The reality is we do have a needy and wounded inner child; how can we deal with it in a healthy way where we can keep dignity, self-respect, and strength?

This is a major piece of inner work for a man to do. And though it can be done alone or within a relationship, it is best done in a supervised environment, working with a good therapist. What I can do here is outline the basic process. The work focuses around the second (belly), third (solar plexus), and fourth (heart) chakras. We have to develop the third charka—our power and self-reliance—in a way that is integrated with our heart and simultaneously embraces our inner child and our needs without being taken over by them. A good way to start this process is to start giving the inner child space by talking about these feelings. It brings you to a new level of vulnerability and honesty. As you do this, there starts a process of separation and dis-identification inside: there is now an adult in you who is present with a new level of detachment and maturity, and who can talk about your needs and your inner child.

This adult consciousness is an aspect of the third chakra and the sixth chakra. You begin to feel a new level of self-reliance and a sense of standing on your own two feet. Now, instead of negating your emotional needs or your inner child, you are taking care of them in a more healthy way. You become the parent to your own inner child. As this happens it 'turns down the volume' of those needs. Through this there is now space for the adult in you and the adult in your partner to meet. This creates a more healthy relationship, where there are two self-reliant adults who are meeting, two adults who each have a needy inner child and who are parenting their own inner children. On the one side this creates freedom and independence between the two of you, and at the same time a deeper intimacy and communication.

As third chakra strength grows, and the potency of individuality opens, the energy becomes available to move from the third chakra to the heart. You discover the strength and courage to love deeply.

There is a collective illusion that love is a natural state to us and that our heart just naturally opens to the person we love. For the majority of us, particularly men, though we do love, **our heart is behind a protective wall**. It takes the strength of the solar plexus to give us the courage to open and become vulnerable. So the capacity for deeper love is a direct reflection of the integration of the strength and power of the solar plexus with the heart chakra.

This creates a problem for many Indigo Souls. Many of them don't really want to work with power. We have seen so much darkness associated with power—abuse of power, selfishness, and egoism—that we want spirituality to be gentle, loving, and kind. But this imbalance creates the problems mentioned above. And then we wonder why our relationships are so messy, why there is so much dependency, why we are getting hurt so much. So to move up into love we need to look downwards and make friends with our inner child and our solar plexus, and integrate our needs and our power. Then we get the best from these two charkas: the warmth, sensuality, and intimacy that the belly can bring, and the power and individuality of the solar plexus—all brought into our heart as a mature capacity for loving.

• *What does this work on my solar plexus entail? Becoming independent, having my own job, earning my own money, or what?*

Certainly all of those things, but it also entails more than that. It entails learning to stand for yourself, learning to be strong in what you want and what you feel. It has a lot to do with having the courage to live your truth, the courage to step out of the box of security that most of us live in, to take risks, to jump into the new. It means the courage to allow confrontation when it is necessary, and not to collapse because of the fear of confrontation. And there is another level as well, perhaps an even more important level. It has to do with confronting in ourselves the deep wounds of shame and unworthiness we carry. These patterns are very destructive; they sabotage us in so many ways. So, to mature the solar plexus means to find the courage to face and explore and work with our feelings of unworthiness and shame, and to heal them. This leads us to a new and healthy sense of self-worth and inner dignity.

• *You say the world is dominated by the solar plexus part, and we are changing to the heart, but are you sure about that? When I look at a lot of what is going on in the world it doesn't seem we are changing.*

Certainly, when you look at the world and what is going on, it does make one wonder, doesn't it? It does make you wonder if we are going backwards. But yes, I do believe that we are changing for the better. The process seems to move two steps forward and one back. And though I certainly do see a lot of misuse of power, selfishness, and ego in the world, I see a great deal of goodness that is emerging. I see a great number of gentle and conscious souls that are on the planet right now. And I see that it is because of the presence of this goodness that the density that is there is highlighted.

I am thinking back to not that long ago in America, when everyone carried a gun, or a knife. The smallest slight led to violence. Thank goodness these things are becoming a lot less prevalent in many parts of the world. That has changed so much. We are learning to talk about our differences instead of just act violently on them. We are beginning to think more inclusively instead of just selfishly. We are developing a humane and caring value system that is beginning to affect not just our personal lives, but is being incorporated into our collective ideas, our laws and legal system. So, on a larger level I see great strides in humankind moving from the solar plexus to the heart.

But I would like to hear more from you. Why do you not feel that we are developing this heart quality?

I used to believe in the inherent goodness of people, and that the world could evolve into a place of friendship and beauty. But I've become more and more pessimistic. What is happening in the world today, especially within the Muslim cultures, seems like they are going backwards, not evolving forwards. It seems like Indigos are happening in the West but not in the Muslim world. Do you think this is true? And if so, can we ever create a better planet as a whole with this division?

There are many parts to your question, so I want to address them one by one. First, I think Indigos are happening everywhere, that it's a stream that is coming in and entering the entire planet, not just some particular countries. In countries that are more restrictive, the Indigos may be less visible and are under greater tension. It is not uncommon to find disturbed Indigos and the resultant acting-out behaviors. Many extreme behaviors we see in the world today result from the Indigo spirit under stress.

Second, I see the problems we are having between the Arab-Muslim world and the Western world as a reflection of the evolutionary steps that we are taking. The interconnectedness that I spoke of earlier is bringing cultures into collision like never before. Many fixed and rigidified ideas and cultural patterns are being challenged to change. Beliefs and lifestyles that have been established for centuries are being disturbed. Naturally there is going to be friction. And it is in the nature of the psyche to make a 'last stand' fight rather than change.

Third, let's make some distinctions. There is the Islamic religion based upon the Koran; there is the Palestinian people and the difficult situation there with Israel; and there are the fundamentalists and extremists.

Let's start first with the Muslim tradition. There are vast numbers of Muslims around the world living beautiful lives based upon the deep and meaningful teachings of the Koran. Most of these people don't make it into the news, so we mostly hear about those who are disturbed. However, as with all established traditions, the teachings were given in a certain cultural situation. Things change. And now there are tremendous challenges the Muslim culture is facing on how to adapt to the new times.

If we look at the Palestinian situation we see a dislocated peoples crammed into a small area of refugee camps. There was a study done with rats that if the population density has the right amount of space, say, five rats per 10 meters (I don't remember the exact numbers), the rats live essentially in peace with one another. But if you compress the space, say, to 10 rats per meter, then violence, aggression, and psychological disturbance rise proportionally. Add to this compression the many other problems the Palestinians are facing—the many other social, economic and political difficulties—with the resultant psychological stress and disturbance, and you have a recipe for disaster.

And then, we have the fundamentalist mentality, a mentality that by the way is happening in all cultures. Fundamentalist thinking, under whatever name, is an incapacity to grow and change with a changing world. It is a reflection of deep disturbances in the psyche. It is a rigidity of the third eye, coupled with an intense emotionality that creates tunnel vision and fanaticism.

Even though this fundamentalism looks as if we are regressing, not progressing, I see it as a last gasp of the old Piscean mentality. When something is coming towards its end, it fights vehemently to hold on to what it has known.

There is one more thing I would like to address here. I think that as a planet, as a whole we are in the midst of some very major teachings about how we use our power, how we relate to others, our interconnectedness, our values, how we communicate, etc. I believe that many of these 'incomplete learnings' are being played out and expressed through the Muslim world.

The Middle-East is an immense focal point of all kinds of collective forces: economic, religious, social, ideological, and cultural. We have tremendous financial forces focused there because of the oil. This brings in the interests of global corporations, and their roots in our Western cultures with their out-of-balance over-emphasis on materialism. Then we have three world religions meeting in one spot, each with its own interests and attitudes. And then we have the Jewish situation and history with all its ramifications, particularly those originating from WW II. This is a lot of vested interests and powerful forces at work focused upon a very small space.

I believe that to solve the problems between the Muslim and Western world it is going to require all of us, both as individuals and collectively, to expand our vision and take responsibility for the part we play. Each of us needs to see how we are part of a larger picture, and how our attitudes, beliefs, behaviors, and lifestyles affect and are affecting the whole. We need to move into global thinking and responsibility.

And the last thing I want to address is what I consider a New Age illusion: that the New Age means we become more loving, harmonious, and wise, and therefore things go so much easier. Every expansion of awareness means we are dealing with greater forces of ourselves and life. So an expansion of awareness is also an expansion of power and the need for greater responsibility and wise use of that power.

So to sum up, in spite of all the problems and challenges in the world today, I do feel hopeful about the direction things are taking.

• *I feel I am an Indigo Soul and can very much relate to what you are saying. I also realize through your talk I am not alone with it, that there are many of us. The ques-*

tion arises: what do I do now with my everyday life? I lost my job recently, and I feel I lost it because of my Indigo nature.

In what ways do you feel that your Indigo nature caused you to lose your work and to not be able to fit in and integrate?

There are two ways. One has to do with my sensitivity. I feel and sense many things that others don't feel. And the second way is I am dealing with pain and wounds from my childhood that are still influencing the way that I deal with daily life.

You know, a lot of Indigo Souls feel like outsiders. You feel like you don't fit, you don't feel integrated in the environment, and because you are sensitive you feel the aggressions, the undercurrents, the 'stuff' that is going on that nobody is addressing and that people keep perpetuating. This makes it very hard on you.

So a lot of Indigo Souls are, unfortunately, often on the fringe of society, though that certainly is not all Indigos. There are many Indigo Souls that are well integrated and successful, but there are many who are struggling to fit in. So it is difficult right now for you and for many of us. One way of dealing with this is to stop trying to fit it. There is a beautiful expression, "A leader creates a world that others want to belong to." Instead of focusing on the world you don't belong to, begin to take note of the world that you do belong to. It is a beautiful world. It is a new world. It is a fresh springtime of energies that are emerging. And as you pay attention to this world you will find many like-minded souls in it.

I would also say to you don't take it so personally. It is very easy to think "Oh, I have a problem," "I am messed up because of my mother and my father," or whatever. And yes, because you are sensitive you have wounds from your upbringing, so you are challenged to heal those wounds. And you are challenged to find your value, to find your strength, to find your voice, to find your truth. So in that sense, do your inner work. A lot of us tip toe around our wounds for years, hoping maybe they are just nothing and they'll go away if we don't pay them any attention and just focus on the positive. At a certain point we recognize that our wounds are there and that we need to deal with them. Then we take the bull by the horns, choose to do the deep inner work of healing our past, and jump in and do it. From your question I sense you are ready to jump in and do this work now.

And you also asked: "What do I do with my everyday life?" First, remember that we are pioneers. I spoke earlier of these ships that break through the ice as they move in the North Sea. You are an icebreaker, pioneering a new way of being. Although that is hard on you, that is part of the job you were hired on for.

One part of our job comes about through the friction of the Old meeting the New. So we have a lot to learn about taking care of our self in this difficult situation. We have to learn to handle not being understood or being judged by finding a new self-reliance in ourselves. We have to learn to handle our unusual level of sensitivity, and how to bring our selves back to balance when we feel overwhelmed or bombarded by things that are normal, even enjoyable, to others.

In a way you can think of daily life as a kind of toughness training for your soul. If you remain so sensitive without learning to handle it you cannot manage. Many Indigo Souls need to get stronger and tougher, while keeping their sensitivity and their loving hearts. Imagine that the situations in your daily life that are difficult are something different than they appear. Think of all these difficult people and energies as being Zen masters in disguise: as your mother, your partner, the clerk in the store, who are going to hit you hard on the head with their Zen sticks until you learn how to handle it.

And the last thing is to recognize the importance of the work you are doing now for the Indigos who come later and for the culture as a whole. Many of us Indigo adults have it so much harder in our role as icebreakers, but because of our work the Indigo kids are so much healthier and can manifest so much more of their Indigo nature. We are laying the foundations of the new culture; it is a very worthwhile task.

5

The Purpose of Indigo Souls

The Sense of 'Calling' and 'Purpose'

One of the most important forces inside of Indigo Souls is their sense of 'calling' or 'purpose.' It can be felt in many ways: you may have a sense that you are here for a reason, or that you have something to do, or that you have something to unfold in yourself, or that you have something to contribute to the world. Whatever its form, this calling is often one of the strongest driving forces within Indigos. In many ways it may be the central point around which their life revolves.

In the beginning this may not be very clear. There may just be a vague sense of longing or desire. There maybe a general sense of, "Oh, I would like to do something more meaningful in my life." Or in many cases it is felt not as a feeling of calling, but as a feeling of dissatisfaction. You are unhappy with a mundane life, with living in a box. And even that is not often very clear; it may be just felt as restlessness or a general dissatisfaction, or perhaps a light depression.

In whatever way it is felt, this sense of meaning is at the core of who you are. You cannot just live your life without meaning and purpose. You cannot just live selfishly. You can certainly live a 'normal' life; normal meaning having a family, going to work, etc., but within this situation there is a need for doing things in a way that uplifts your spirit, that matters to your heart. Things have to have a higher value that gives you the feeling that you are contributing to making the world a little bit better.

That sense of making the world better is core to your purpose and your calling. Perhaps your way of making the world better is simple: not doing other people harm, or helping people be a little happier. Or perhaps your sense of purpose takes a more powerful form: you desire to work in a profession that helps people, or to work with the environment, or a charity, or research for the greater good. There is a fundamental desire to make a positive contribution. That feeling becomes more and more powerful over time.

Some people are born with it as a powerful passion. In other people it gradually unfolds. In either case your life becomes measured according to that standard. If you are living your life according to your calling, it brings a certain fulfillment. There is a feeling of, "I am living a right life, I am living what I am here for." If you are not living according to that, there is an emptiness, as if there is something missing, an 'existential dissatisfaction.'

A related theme that is often very challenging is that many Indigo Souls have a sense of purpose and direction, but cannot find a form or an outlet for it that satisfies them. This can be a source of great suffering. It's as if you sense that there is so much that you have in you, so much that you would like to do, but you don't know what to do with it. Or perhaps you know what to do with it but you can't seem to bring it through.

For example, I know so many people trained in some form of self-development work—bodywork, Reiki, psychotherapy, an alternative healing method, etc.,—who can't find enough clients to make a living at it and end up working at some job that doesn't satisfy them. This discrepancy between what you know inside versus what you can live and express in the outside world is often great. This can be a source of deep discontent and pain. Your desire to be all that you can be is so strong and your awareness very sharp and keen; if you are not living that ideal you are painfully aware of it, and you suffer when you are not living to your potential or your optimum.

We've spoken about this before, that your consciousness is of the new, of the future, but your personality is of the old. You hold images and feelings of new ways of being, but the personality that exists within is a Piscean personality; not only Piscean but also a personality formed from instincts that go back millions of years and is still very primitive. It has a lot of lower chakra activity in it: it is selfish, power-orientated and competitive (third chakra), fearful (base chakra), and greedy (second chakra). It has a closed and judgmental mind (sixth chakra), and the emotions are very strong and volatile (dominant emotional body).

Many Indigo Souls are excruciatingly aware that there are two people in them: their higher consciousness, which is more open, vital, vibrant, and uplifted; and their personality, which is dense, emotional, limited, and closed. Being an Indigo Soul in a Piscean personality and body is not easy! This is a huge discrepancy: what you know in your innermost consciousness is not what you can live in your normal thinking, emotions, or behavior.

To picture this, imagine that you are a world-class racing driver, and you are given an old, beaten up car that hardly moves anymore. You know what you are capable of doing and should be able to do with it, but with that car you are not very successful when you try to drive it.

This is the root cause of a lot of our struggle: we are not living or being the person that we know we can be, that we want to be. This can create a deep inner anguish. In addition, your Critic points a finger at all your faults and then beats you up. Most Indigo Souls have strong Critics, with the result that they suffer from a sense of inferiority. You feel like you are not enough, that you are not doing enough, that you are not good enough. And then your Pusher, your 'Spiritual Pusher,' complicates it even more by making you work even harder. The result is that you end up with a lot of tensions. And no matter how hard you work, you never fully succeed. What a vicious circle! The Critic finds fault, the Pusher pushes, the Critic finds it not enough, you push more,…

It is because of this discrepancy between the ideal and the real that one of the central teachings for Indigo Souls is self love: being gentle towards your self, walking the path softly. Have your ideals. Aspire towards them. And yet realize that you will never fully reach them. You will always fall short, and that is fine, you are not meant to reach them; you are meant to stretch towards them, but not to reach them. When you realize that, something inside relaxes. Then you can love yourself for being just another imperfect human being on the planet, instead of loving yourself only when you have attained sainthood. So in a sense we can say that your purpose, or one part of your purpose, is to be reaching towards ideals—not reaching ideals, but reaching towards them.

Part of Your Purpose is to be a Transformer of the World Matrix

By reaching towards ideals you are transforming various energies and patterns that sit within your mind and psyche and energy field. By wrestling with these patterns they are gradually shifting and transforming inside of you. We spoke about the Matrix earlier and how, though we feel ourselves as separate, isolated persons struggling with our separate issues, in reality we are part of the great Matrix, the great field of energy of the Earth.

The Matrix has certain vibratory patterns and structures woven in it. Those energy patterns operate like a 'cookie cutter' in which they stamp or mold certain parts of our psyche.

Though you know this already, I want to again emphasize the point because it is so central to the expansion of consciousness process we are all in. When we were born and grew up, our psyche was being energetically molded by patterns within the collective Matrix. Those patterns are in you, and those patterns are in millions and millions of other people. And not only are they in you, they are linked: my patterns are linked to your patterns through energetic threads that are invisible to the naked eye but are threads linking us together in the energy world. So, as you are aspiring and stretching and reaching towards these ideals, what you are doing is transforming a piece of the collective energy pattern. It is not just your own energy transforming; you are actually transforming a piece of the world Matrix.

In a sense, one aspect of your purpose is to be a 'human transformer.' You are here, as the old alchemists used to say, "to change lead into gold," and that transformation is happening within your own body and energy field. As I mentioned earlier, by transforming it within yourself you are lifting the Matrix a little bit. Millions and millions of people work on exactly the same issues that you are working on—you are working on yours and they are working on theirs—and together we are transforming this strand of energy that is woven through the collective. As you do that, the collective energy starts vibrating at a higher frequency. It starts holding a new, lighter, more life-supportive vibration. You begin to embody the ideals and the higher frequencies of energy that are living in your soul, and you start bringing them down into this plane of reality.

So we could say that your purpose has several core factors:

1. To be a human transformer.

You do that by working on your issues and patterns, your 'stuff.' A lot of us feel that "if I am a spiritual person, then I should feel good, and I should be happy; then I have arrived." I would like to say to you that what you actually should be doing is on a regular basis hitting stuff, and working with it, and transforming it. So the more imperfections you hit, the more stuff you hit, the more you are contributing to the light, to the building of the new. I am especially telling your Critic this, so that your Critic can give you a pat on the back every time you hit another imperfection. Then you can say: "Great, I have earned another ten points in terms of being a planetary energy transformer."

2. Holding higher and higher frequencies of energy.

Your soul holds immense qualities and frequencies of energies. What we are doing is transforming lower vibratory frequencies of energy into higher frequencies of energy. An essential part of this process is bringing the qualities of the soul, which open through the Crown chakra, down into the core channel, into the chakras and the body. We call this process 'holding light.' You are here to hold light in yourself as an energy being.

3. Holding and living new ways of being.

Your soul holds ideals of new ways of being. You hold pictures of the new forms of relating, which are more heartful, more authentic, and have more depth. You hold pictures of new forms of communication, where we speak in more honest and authentic ways. You hold images of new ways of using power that have more heart and more respect. You hold ideals of the new relationship between the soul and the body, between the Spirit and the Earth. You hold ideas concerning almost every area of life: healing, the body, business, child rearing, family, education, science, religion, etc.

These new ideals are held in you as new paradigms and ways of being. These ideals are thought forms held in the higher frequencies of energies that surround the Earth. And these thought forms are gradually penetrating into our conscious-ness. They are gradually penetrating into our thoughts and into our behavior. We begin to behave differently, according to this new way of being. And ultimately, as you behave in that new way and other people behave in that new way, we cre-ate in the world a new state and way of being. And when we (we in the collective sense of many, many people) are doing this, what we build is a new civilization built on these new ideals and these new ways of being.

Your Unique Task

Each one of us has all of these ideals within us, but there are certain ideals that are particularly important for us. You could say that we become specialists in these areas. Perhaps your particular task is to learn to relate in a new way, or perhaps it is to relate with nature and ecology in a new way, or perhaps it is to contribute to understanding the mind-body-energy relationship in a new way. It brings great fulfillment to you when you understand your particular area of focus.

As you find it you also discover the level of involvement for you in it. For some of us it is to work with that on a day-to-day level in our personal life. And for some of us it is to make that into a career, or some sort of highly active calling. The main thing is that once you are 'living your dharma' as they say in the East, your life has purpose and meaning in a way that nothing else brings.

As you find your task it brings you into connection with members of your soul family who are connected to that task. What we see is that souls travel through incarnations like clusters of grapes. A group of souls with similar energies, themes, and vibrations will incarnate more or less together in a similar time or location. As you come into connection with your own soul and your soul purpose, you start meeting these other related souls. You share a state of deep connectedness and understanding, of rapport, of mutual support, and love. As you awaken to your soul nature you realize that there are many other souls that are interwoven with you. You begin to link hands, so to speak, on an energetic and soul level. That is deeply rewarding and supportive.

As you emerge into your soul purpose you do what we call 'stepping between worlds.' That means we are all born into a family, a neighborhood, a society. That is one world that we live in. Some Indigo Souls find themselves well connected with family and friends—you are the lucky ones. A great many Indigo Souls feel disconnected, you don't feel like you fit; you feel separate, and in many ways you don't belong, even though you try. As you start waking up to your soul purpose, you start meeting people of a similar vibration and quality. You begin to step out of trying to belong to the old world, and you start belonging to the new world. Then you exist in both worlds, but your nurturance comes, to a great degree, from the new one. And ultimately you are here to build this new world.

Here at the beginning of the 21st century, it is sometimes hard for us to see what we are building. You are familiar with what is called 'The hundredth monkey effect.' It means you don't see anything changing, then suddenly it just takes one little extra thing that looks like nothing, and things start changing radically. We don't notice that the effort that we are putting in is bringing an effect, and then suddenly things change so fast. So we need to be patient and gentle with our self, trust our calling, and follow something that is bigger than us. Though your mind may sometimes say, "It's too much, it isn't real," follow your calling, trust in your sense of purpose. Trust in the capacities that you sense are possible in you even though they are not yet fully there. Your soul is stretching you. Your soul is asking you to jump. Your soul is asking you to take risks. Trust in it, it is worth it. Be relaxed with it, be gentle. It is okay not to be perfect, and at the same time keep jumping. After a while you love the feeling of living on the edge.

Questions & Answers

• *I do not find my sense of purpose. I find myself looking for what to do. And on the other side there is a strong longing to be spiritual and to connect to people on a spiri-*

tual level. I find myself very much struggling. And I feel that I still have to transform a lot of stuff.

That is the main job anyway, that is the main purpose: to transform our 'stuff!'

But what I am hearing is that your calling to find a form is strong, but you are not finding it yet, is that right?

Yes.

That is a painful place.

I have these spiritual ideals that I want to reach, but I find myself continually in the same old pattern. There is a spiritual longing and interest, but I don't get it together.

My sense is that you are hitting some of your core patterns. Core patterns are deep recurrent patterns and habits that keep tripping us up and dropping our consciousness. My experience is that when there is a pattern, behind it is a soul teaching, and behind that is an unfolding of a state of Essence, or quality of the soul. So what feels like a problem is a door to the soul. My suggestion is to commit to looking more deeply into those patterns. Probably there are things that have happened in your past that are keeping you from stepping into your energy. You are reminding me that at many points on the path we go through what we call a 'spiritual crisis.' A spiritual crisis is when the discrepancy between the ideal and the real, or between our future calling and our past patterns becomes such a tension that it catalyses a jump to happen. A new focus, a new intensity, a new totality emerges. It usually happens through intensely confronting ourselves and doing a powerful piece of inner work. My guess is that you have done some work already on this issue, and there is more to do. So rather than being disappointed with your self or the inner work process because you haven't arrived yet, jump in there with totality and take another big step on the journey.

• *I get inklings of what I am here to do, but then life's practical circumstances stop me from doing it.*

For some people their purpose is a given: it is there and it is clear. For most people, finding their purpose is like a game of hide and seek. It is something you have to work at. Finding your purpose becomes a central part of your purpose. You sense that it is there, and then it is gone. It gives a twinkle, you reach for it, and then it is beyond your grasp.

But there's a second thing that I sense with you. I sense that you have a strong inner Critic, and that it is standing in front of the doorway saying, "You are not good enough, you can't do that."

Yes. My struggle with my inner Critic is that I go into my head and that cuts me off from my intuition.

Sometimes the Critic can be a great ally if you know how to use it. My guess is that your Critic is pointing at parts of your calling, but you are not daring to say, "Okay I will do them." What do you think?

Yes, there are different things: working with massage, dance, and the body. I feel it is a natural that has been given to me.

So it's actually clear what some aspects of your purpose are; it's just that your inner Critic stops you as well as life's practical circumstances getting in the way. And about the circumstances: to follow one's purpose often requires an almost heroic effort to commit and discipline and focus ourselves. We have many patterns that easily sidetrack us. But if we take the responsibility and commit, then we can do it.

One other thing for you to know: following your purpose isn't always convenient. It doesn't always make money easily or get supported by others. It takes courage and trust to follow your heart and your intuition and go against the normal logic of the mind. Often times you have to go against people or situations around you that deter you. It will take a commitment and a discipline to stay true to your purpose. You will have to find the strength and courage in your self. You might not get a lot of support.

• *My surroundings, and particularly my partner, make it very difficult to exercise my spirituality. I have to fight for the space and time to have it.*

An important part of your spiritual purpose as a woman is to work on the man in your life! I have to be very honest with you. Speaking as a man, we are stubborn; we are arrogant; we are full of masks over our shame, insecurities and fears; we think we know it all; and that we don't have any need to change. In so many ways women are more advanced spiritually. You are more open, you are willing to look at yourself, and you are more in touch with your feelings, your vulnerability, and a deeper level of honesty. We men need to learn that from you. But we don't think we need to learn that from you. And in most cases we don't want to learn it from you. But we have called you into our life because we need to learn it. What do you think of that?

I am sick and tired of trying to explain it and prove it and getting so much resistance, walls, attacks...

It *is* very difficult. We men *are* very difficult. What to say, it is the truth. So you need a lot of patience, a lot of skill, and the right dose of emotional explosions at the right moments.

(Audience) She would like to have the permission to explode occasionally.

Well, then I give you the permission! Part of your spiritual purpose is to explode at home to wake up your man!

More realistically, your personality patterns are keeping you protected.

I would describe myself as a diplomat.

Exactly. When I feel you inside, you are a lively, dynamic, and passionate woman. But how much of your passion comes out directly rather than through the filters of diplomacy, etc? My body tells me you are holding back, so where are you holding back?

I can't answer that although it is a crucial question to find the point that is holding back.

I sense a lot of fear in you. And the second thing I sense is the fear of confrontation and engagement. When we speak to people our energy goes out of us and contacts the energy field of the other. But that contact can happen in many ways. For example, my energy can come out of me but it can fall on the ground in front of you and not reach you, or it can go over your left shoulder and not really touch you, or my energy could really come and really meet you and really connect with you. I sense that there is a lot that you can learn about direct meeting. My sense is that some of your holding back has to do with resentments you are holding from the past, from your childhood. That a part of you says: "I am not going to give myself to you."

I pride myself that I keep something back.

Exactly. That gives that part a certain power and satisfaction. But that part is a pattern from the past that is limiting your energy and your ability to engage more constructively and clearly with your partner, or with people in general. Learn more about directly meeting others with your passion and energy. In the beginning it might be emotional and explosive, but that is only in the beginning. After a while the excess heat will burn off, and a new clarity and potency will arise. Then you won't feel like a victim of the limits of your partner or the surroundings. You are limiting yourself. Your patterns are holding you back. It's easy to put the blame on the other or the outside. The outside will always be difficult. But it's what you make of it that matters.

6

The New Archetypes—The Ideals Held in our Higher Levels of Consciousness

I would like to pick up from where we left off in our last talk: exploring the Aquarian archetypes as they unfold through the chakras. We have spoken earlier of how, in the higher level of our consciousness there are contained images of new ways of being. Probably the best way to describe them is to call them 'ideas.' These are ideas that are held in the inner world. They become 'ideals' for us to work toward in this world. These 'ideals' are images or pictures that call to us. We are sensing potentials and possibilities that we are destined to become.

To understand the Aquarian archetypes, imagine that every age of 2160 years is built on foundational ideas and understandings. Over a period of around 2160 years, these ideas and images gradually unfold to define and take shape. Toward the latter part of an age, the ideas and resultant role structures become quite crystallized. To give you an example, most of our mothers and our fathers, and especially our grandmothers and grandfathers, were pretty clear on their role as men or as women. They knew how they should behave and their position in society; it was a pretty clear-cut set of definitions and behaviors. But in our generation that has been shaken up. This is particularly so for women. How many women these days are content to be under the thumb of their men? Certainly there are some, but the greater majority of women today would find this unacceptable. This is because there is a new image of womanhood that is held in our consciousness.

It is as if you carry a picture that, though not necessarily clear in your normal mind, is clear in your higher consciousness. This picture calls to you to become it. That picture, and the energy that's contained within it, is powerful. It stirs you, makes you restless, makes you discontented with the old, makes you rebel against limiting things, makes you seek for new ways. These kinds of images exist at many different levels of the psyche. Each chakra is unfolding a number of different images concerned with its related aspect of life.

The Base Chakra

Letting go of the Piscean shame and guilt toward our body

I would like to begin with the Base chakra. One of the biggest shifts in the Base chakra for the New Humanity is the 'spiritual celebration of the body and of nature.' The Christian model of the last 2000 years was based on a denial of the body. It was as if the body was not holy or spiritual. It was something to be pushed away and that we were in judgment towards.

This old attitude was not bad; it served a necessary evolutionary purpose that was part of a developmental step of the Piscean Age. The denial of the body served us by helping us move beyond being consumed by the animal passions. By judging and condemning the body, we began to focus toward a higher consciousness. So, though this condemnation has created many problems for us, when seen in an evolutionary sense it has served its purpose.

But something new is now happening. The archetype that is now unfolding concerning the body is to celebrate and enjoy the body, and to see it as divine—a temple housing the soul. We are learning to enjoy life as a sensual delight, with consciousness. To do that we have to work through the shame and guilt that we carry from our past. The Piscean past created a feeling of wrongness about the senses and the body. This is still a powerful force in our psyches. We feel guilty about our senses and we judge our body. Part of our learning now is to let go of that.

We are learning now not only to be in the senses, but also to be consciously in the senses. It is very easy just to go unconscious and have an 'orgy of the senses.' It is another thing to hold consciousness, to remain aware, and through doing so to hold the fineness of one's Essence and to let that move in and through the body.

This state is probably best reflected in the widespread emergence of Tantra. Most of us are familiar with the word 'Tantra.' Tantra is about conscious sexuality. Up until a few years ago, it was almost non-existent except in a few very small corners of the planet. Now it is common; Tantra workshops and trainings are happening everywhere, and its prevalence is growing rapidly. I believe that Tantra has only just begun to make itself felt. It is still an unrealized ideal.

Imagine that for the last 2000 years the majority of human beings would go to the church, condemn their bodies as sinful, and pray to be forgiven. Of course, this sounds ridiculous to our Piscean belief structure, but maybe as things progress into this New Age we might have Tantric churches ringing their bells on Sunday. I believe that Tantra will become integrated and widespread as more and more people embrace this life-affirmative approach of celebrating the body.

The recognition of the soul as a separate entity from the body

There is a second 'new' idea connected to the body that is one of the keynotes of new consciousness. (It's actually a very old idea that is reappearing in a new way.) It is the recognition of the soul as separate from the body. We are coming to perceive our selves as spiritual entities who temporarily inhabit our bodies. I believe that in the next few years a deeper understanding of the mechanisms whereby the soul interfaces with the body will emerge. Though this 'Science of the Soul' has, in the past, been the domain of religion or spirituality, I believe that in the future it will come more under the domain of science.

This growing awareness of the body as separate from the soul is currently being expressed in our culture in an interesting way. Though it is occurring at a mass-consciousness level, it is still a significant indication of this unfolding understanding. It is the trend toward changing our body to meet our desires through plastic surgery. Through surgical and other methods, we are able to make the body look a certain way. And this is just the beginning. I'm sure you are aware of the research into growing new organs and new limbs. Where we are going in the future will be quite radical and could be called 'Designer Bodies.' You will go down to your body shop, choose the changes you would like, and they will easily change your body according to your desires.

Now many of us in the New Age are shocked at this, at what we would call the lack of naturalness, the lack of organicness, the artificiality, and superficiality. Yet, as the Aquarian energies are coming in, this trend is happening around the world and is growing rapidly. We recently had in this seminar room here in Germany a young Brazilian couple in their early 20s. She said that she had recently had a nose job, "I didn't like my nose, so I got a new one," and then the boyfriend said, "Oh yes, and so did I." Most of the group members were shocked. And then she said: "I can't wait to get back to Brazil, I am going to get a whole bunch of other new things." She was so excited about it.

We didn't realize here in Germany that in Brazil everybody is changing the body. It is relatively inexpensive, and it has become the 'in' thing to do. It is so in many countries in South America, and in North America it is becoming more common. Though many of us here in Europe are a little slower, it is catching on. I cannot say whether it is a good thing or a bad thing. What I can say is that, though we will in some ways misuse every new thing, it doesn't mean that the new is bad. Rather we need to see it as part of the direction evolution is taking.

Genetic engineering will extend our life span and solve many emotional and mental sufferings

Most of us are aware of the significance of what is happening in the world of genetic research. You probably have heard that scientists have decoded the human genome. What that means is they have mapped the DNA blueprint for building a human being. Gradually, they will know exactly which gene makes your eyes blue, or your hair brown; which gene makes your heart healthy, or not healthy. We will soon be curing diseases that have plagued human beings forever. I expect that the average lifespan of people will be extended tremendously through this genetic work. And also that many of the problems that we suffer from today—emotionally and mentally as well as physically—will be solved.

A certain percentage of our struggles on the path of inner development are due to genetic programming that does not permit the fuller capacities of the soul to express. Some of these limitations can be changed through genetics. Imagine, for example, that you did not have to wrestle with your insecurities or fears day in and day out. A lot of the reason we feel insecure or fearful has to do with genetic programming from evolution which is millions of years old and doesn't serve us anymore now. Or imagine the anger that so many of us struggle with. This also could be resolved. These and many other emotional and mental patterns are the result of inherited instinctual biological programs in the brain and glands that are not working for us anymore and are not needed or appropriate for a 21st century human being.

I think one of the greatest accelerants to spiritual growth on the planet is going to be genetic research. I know that is shocking to many New Agers, because many of us believe that it is through meditation, eating healthy, and living a spiritual life that our spiritual development should happen. And on one hand that is true. But if you look at the unfolding trends that are happening on the planet—genetic research and the developments in the fields of chemistry, biology, and medicine—these things are going to have a very large effect on our emotional, mental, and spiritual well-being.

If someone offered you a pill that would remove your anger, remove your insecurities, give you more vitality, give you the body that you have always wanted, and as well told you that you would live disease-free, tell me wouldn't you take it? I would, and I would be jumping to do so. I think that is what is going to become available in steps and stages down the road in the not-too-distant future.

The Unfolding Archetypes of the Second Chakra

Let's move on from the body to the next series of archetypes and images: those connected to the second chakra and the unfolding archetypes of the family.

If we look historically at the family structure, we see significant evolutionary changes throughout its history. Initially we human beings lived in tribes in extended family groupings. It was not uncommon for a woman to have a dozen children. There would be many such families living together, and there would be many children around. The children would, in essence, have many substitute parents, many aunts, and uncles. They had a tremendous support system. Over time we moved into the nuclear family—the husband and wife. This is the main family grouping today. In earlier times, nuclear families tended to remain in their original locations, so there were aunts, uncles, and grandparents around. These days more and more people are moving away from where they grew up, so there is less of a blood-family support system available to the adults and the kids.

This has resulted in a great deal of psychological disturbance for children. Although a child needs a primary mother and a primary father to bond with, a child also needs many different people to be in relationship with. A child needs many people whom it gets love from, whom it communicates with, whom it models on, and with whom it shares with. If a child doesn't get this, it creates a kind of lack in our psyche that we then fill with substitutes, such as food, drink, drugs, sex, or preoccupation with material objects.

As the previous form of extended family grouping is disappearing, we are seeing people developing new ways of linkages and interconnectedness that are outside of the family grouping. For example, mothers are getting together with other mothers in mothers' groups, or in other forms of extended child-support groups. If we project this into the future, what we see happening is completely new forms of extended family groupings that will be taking place. In other words, we see new forms of 'community,' or the sense of community, new ways of finding interconnectedness with the world around us.

The last 50 years saw many experiments with communities and communes, one of the most successful being the Kibbutz's in Israel. I believe that these forms of community will become more and more common. They will take many shapes. It doesn't necessarily mean that everyone lives together on a single piece of property. More probably it may mean that people live separate. But through the connectedness of the Internet, telephones, and computers, the linkage of community will be intensified greatly.

On a more personal note, so many people suffer because they feel disconnected. Indigo Souls are still very much in the minority in terms of numbers, so this feeling of separation is often strong for you. And this can lead to a great deal of suffering. It creates a strong longing in you to find 'kindred souls.' You are looking for people of like mind and heart. You are looking for people who you can meet on a deeper level and who share that connection with you.

One of the most common forms that this need for connection takes is through small spiritual or inner development centers. These small growth centers are emerging everywhere. In Germany alone, we have a two-inch thick book containing addresses of growth centers offering programs and seminar space, with thousands of centers listed. This emergence of centers is happening in response to many factors. These places fulfill not only our need for spiritual development, but also our need for community, extended family, and emotional connectedness.

As an Indigo Soul it is important for you to find ways to emotionally connect to other like souls. And know that none of these ways will be perfect. There are too many frictions still in our personalities. The old forms of relating are still present and we have not yet evolved the new. There will still be many frictions that make connecting incomplete or difficult. Yet, even with all the difficulties, your need for connection remains, and it will be important for you to find ways to reach out to others. Many Indigo Souls, though certainly not all, live isolated and separate lives. The lack of resonance with others, the lack of understanding, and the pain associated with 'dense personalities' make them withdraw.

Though you certainly need time alone, you also need connection and community. I would encourage you to find ways of reaching out and connecting. This is an important part of the next step for humanity: becoming aware of our interconnectedness and learning new ways of interrelating. This growing awareness of interconnectedness and the resultant new forms of relating are essential for the emerging group consciousness that is such a central part of the New Humanity.

The New Science of Conscious Parenting

One of the things we see emerging as part of this process is a new form of parenting to help children develop. We could call it, for lack of better words, 'conscious parenting.' It is clear to psychologists that the majority of emotional, mental, and relationship problems that people deal with in adult life originate from things that happened in childhood. The best way to solve a lot of problems of adults is to bring up children in a more healthy way, so we don't have these problems in the first place. The new form of parenting can do this.

One of the keynotes of this new form of parenting is parent training. I believe that in the future, parents will undergo an intensive form of self-development training to prepare them to be parents. In most countries if you want to drive a car you have to go through driver's education. The process of driving a car is a great deal simpler than learning to develop a human being into a whole and healthy person. Yet anybody can have a child without training. There is a belief that everyone just naturally has the inherent knowledge to bring up his or her child in a healthy way, and knows how to support the child to grow into a mature and healthy adult. What we end up having is neurotic people taking healthy children and turning them into neurotic and disturbed adults.

The human psyche is one of the most complex things on Earth. It is one of the most delicate mechanisms. Ideally a parent should have the training equivalent to a brain surgeon's to bring up a child into a healthy adult. I believe that in the future, this need will be recognized and some type of parent-training programs will be developed.

Essential to that training will be the inner development and maturity of the parents themselves. A child's psyche is like a sponge. It drinks from the energy of the parents. It models on the parents—not just on the parents' outer actions and words, but on the subtle energies, thoughts, and feelings that move within the parents. In essence, to get healthy children you need healthy parents. Parents who, in addition to their own emotional health, have the knowledge and skills for working with a child to help him or her become whole. We believe that these types of programs will become standard in the not-too-distant future. And as part of it, we will end up with some form of parent licensing. We believe that we will see as a result of such a program a generation of children that are not broken souls.

What we see through our work with people is that the majority of us adults are, to some extent, crippled because of our childhood. But because almost everyone is crippled, we don't know that we are crippled; it seems to be the normal state. A lot of what we work on under the name of inner development or spiritual growth is emotional issues resulting from things that got harmed in us when we were children. We are trying to fix things that should not have been broken in the first place!

All of us who are involved in inner development know the pain and difficulties of working intensely on issues and yet not ever really completing or going beyond them. It is painful for me to say this, but to a certain degree some of the issues we struggle with, no matter how hard we work, we will not get through. It is like if you have a beautiful Chinese vase, and you drop it. Yes, you can glue it together again, but it is never going to be the same. And that is what has happened to us. In most cases it wasn't done out of maliciousness, it was done out of ignorance. But the result is that all of us are struggling with emotional, energetic, and mental issues that we don't need to be struggling with if we had been brought up better. We may learn to put the vase back together again, and we may even put it together in a way that it doesn't leak water, but it will have certain weaknesses and blemishes. So if we can alleviate a lot of this breakage by better parenting, it is our responsibility to do so.

(As a side note to all of us 'broken vases,' and speaking especially to your Critic: we are all broken vases, so be gentle with yourself. Don't expect perfection out of yourself because you cannot get there. You are going to limp a bit but you will still reach the mountain top.)

I believe that in the future, governments will put some of the vast amounts of money that currently go into military into child-rearing, parent education, and education in general. And when we do that, the generation that grows up will have an emotional and spiritual wholeness that we can hardly even imagine today. So many of the problems in the world right now result from our development and upbringing. We try all sorts of social, economic, and legal solutions. And though all these things certainly help, the problems still remain. Perhaps one of the best solutions is to bring up the next generation healthy. We can create a much better world in one generation if we were to apply ourselves to creating healthy people. And I believe that we will do this—may be not immediately, but certainly in the not-too-distant future.

Questions & Answers

• *By and large I have a positive and uplifted feeling about what you have said, except for one thing: the aspect of silicon breasts and plastic noses. I believe that my soul chose this body and the issues of this life, even my parents and upbringing, and my body just belongs to that. I think my soul chose this body for a good reason and that shame is part of the learning possibility. If you just operate, you take away the possibility for the soul to get the teachings about shame.*

You see it as part of your soul's learning to get teachings about shame. What if there was a way for you to get those teachings more easily?

But that doesn't happen with operations.

I am not so sure. I have always felt the same as you. I was strongly against all this cosmetic plastic surgery. Then I saw a television show that changed my thinking. It was a show on plastic surgery, showing the actual operations, and also showing interviews with the people about their experience. I remember one young boy of about 14. He had ears that stuck out, extremely so. This poor kid was teased mercilessly and because of it he had developed such a shame and shyness and insecurity about himself. He was carrying such a trauma. Just to go outside and be around people was such a trauma for him. People were always staring at him, laughing at him about his ears.

Then they had an interview with the plastic surgeon showing what a simple operation it was for the ears to come back to normal. They showed the boy going through the operation, and they showed him afterwards with his nice, flat ears. They then interviewed him, and this kid was glowing. He said: "I don't feel like a freak show, I am happy for people to look at me now." It was as if years and years of trauma were taken away from him in one operation. This was the first time I saw plastic surgery as positive for a person. It really gave this boy such a new attitude about himself and his life. I know from therapy just how difficult this type of shame and self-judgment can be to change. That is where I began to turn and see that these things can be very positive.

I feel that what's lacking is some sort of training from the surgeons so that these types of operations can be used properly by people. If people change their noses and breasts there should be some kind of accompanying education to enlighten them about what it does to them and the inherent dangers. I don't see this happening and this is the problem.

I agree with you. These things can be used to enhance one's ego, or they can be used to enhance one's Essence. People need to be helped and taught to connect with their Essence, and then these types of advances can be supportive to one's being, to having a more healthy or suitable vessel for our soul to express itself through. The education process that you are describing will be very important.

I also realize that there will be many abuses of the process as it evolves. People will certainly use plastic surgery for less than perfect reasons. I think that every advance that we make will be abused, and unfortunately that is part of the evolutionary process. It wouldn't surprise me if a lot of this research ends up being funded by sources that I might not morally feel good with. For example, by the military to develop better soldiers. But society in general will reap the rewards of good research. So I think that it is all just part of the process. What most people might not be aware of with the Internet—and I believe the Internet is a great thing—is that it was funded primarily through pornography. Pornography was one of the main forces that created the Internet. So I think it is part of the process that some of the things will be misused and strange things will happen, but the end will be for the overall good.

There is also something else involved here in your initial comment. There is a certain type of spiritual thought that says, "My soul has chosen exactly the perfect body, family, circumstances, and experiences to learn from." This type of thinking would then say: "I have come to this Earth for my soul to learn from this body, and I am this little boy, and my body grew these kinds of ears so I can learn about shame." Many people think this way. Perhaps it is true. But I have another thought. Perhaps the soul comes here and has incredible potential, but actually gets imprisoned and caught in things, such as ears that are like this. For the whole life this soul is only busy with shame. It seems such a waste to struggle so long and painfully for such a thing. If you could move through this shame and resolve it in a more easy and quick way, then the soul could make so much more progress in so many more areas.

So let me put something before us to contemplate. Did the soul choose that body exactly because that body is the best body to learn the teachings, or did the soul just take the best body it could get, but may be it got a less-than-perfect deal?

I'm responding to your question as a mother. As a mother, if my son has these ears, and he has all this pain and comes home crying everyday, can I just tell him, "It is for your inner growth"? What would you do? Ridicule is so painful.

Let me throw you a more shocking example, and let's see what you would do. You know what SPAM is, an unsolicited email. Companies get 2,000,000 email addresses and they send their products out to everybody. One of the largest ones that are out there are companies that advertises penis enhancers, how to make your penis bigger. I used to look at these emails and react with, "These people are sick," until I talked to a woman whose husband had a very small penis. She was very upset, because she said: "When he makes love to me, I don't feel anything, I don't know if he is inside me or not, I have no pleasure at all. I love him, but I am thinking about other men all the time, because I am totally dissatisfied physically." And the man knew this, and felt like such a failure as a man. So what would you suggest to this couple? And women, what would you suggest to your men, if this enhancer were available and healthy? And men, what would you do if you felt your woman was going to leave you just because of two little inches? What would you do in this situation?

(Members of the audience)
I would enhance, it would solve a lot of problems.
I would say try it.
I would take the biggest enlargement available.
It is a question of fit, maybe he should find a woman with a small vagina.
If it is a sexual issue, be connected at your heart level with the husband, and go out and have sex with someone else.

There are many options. But what is clear to me for the first time, as far as we know, choices are being made available to us that we never had before.

Let me take this one step further. If someone said to you, "We can now enhance the length of your life. We have a pill, take it, and you will live an extra 50 years." Would you take it? And let's say you kept looking good as part of the bargain.

It would depend on who else would take it.

I would take it for sure, but I would take it so I would have the time to be aware of the possibility of death, to be aware of what I am really waiting for, to be more completely connected to my Essence, to be aware of what I am really living for. I am not yet aware of my own death, I feel that I live under the illusion that I will live forever.

I am similar to you. I feel that Essence is the most important thing that matters, and how long you live is secondary. I am ten years older than you, and for the first time I have begun to sense old age. I can feel my body starting to wear out. My joints have begun to give me problems, and I start looking at older people in a way that I haven't looked at them before. I see them and think, "I am going to be that way before long." I saw an older woman the other day with osteoporosis, with her back curled right over. I look at her and I thought, "That is not a nice way to live." I don't know what my particular problems with my body will be, and I don't really care about living 100 or 200 years, but I would love to live my last years in a body that is relatively healthy and pain-free, in a body that is not a struggle. I am very happy for medical advances to give me a pain-free life.

Let me throw you a concept that for many New Agers is disturbing. I mentioned it earlier, but I think it went in one ear and out the other. What if your soul didn't choose this body, it just got the pick of the lottery. And by the time it came to your number, all the good ones had gone. So you got a personality and you got a body, and you got a family. And it wasn't what your soul necessarily wanted, but it took what it could get.

Or what if your body and your psyche are designed, to some extent, by random evolutionary forces? And that the soul came down here because it is still an interesting life, but you definitely didn't get a Rolls Royce. Actually my view is more that way. When I look at the structure of the brain, the glands, the mind, the emotions, what I see is that the human vehicle is not very well constructed; it is still relatively primitive, and the soul is struggling with it, is having a hard time with it.

I never thought this way.

No, most people don't. It is not a very comfortable idea.

It makes me angry. It is not just, it is not fair.

I would like to believe that life is fair but when I look around I'm not so sure that fairness is a cosmic principle that Existence abides by.

Yes. And figuring out how does the soul feel in this body. Something feels very tight, as if I am stuck here. On the physical level I don't feel really present here, as if I am not really aware of or in my whole body. Perhaps I need to explore what it means to be present and in my body, and why it feels so tight.

I think your approach to exploring it is right: to explore what is the body, what is the soul, and how are these two interfacing.

And I want to add my own insight regarding this as well as to echo what is said in esoteric work. Esoteric work says the body has been evolved partially through evolutionary forces playing out in nature, and partially through the soul's involvement. That the human body is a construct that it has partially been shaped by, for lack of better words, the great intelligence of the soul, but that it is a far from finished construct; it is still in the process of being developed. Esoterics says that because of this the soul is struggling.

We also believe that the future science will recognize the soul. That we will develop machines to sense the soul as well as being able to sense it directly through our intuitive capacities, and the result will be that we are able to work more directly with the soul. Imagine some of those beautiful moments that you touch so rarely, for example, through meditation. Imagine that those moments could become more regular and solid for you, just through a little adjustment or a little implant. That is what I believe we will develop.

I think the technologies that are coming in terms of changing consciousness are going to blow our minds. Some incredible changes are coming in terms of understanding the body, the psyche, and the soul. The resultant technologies will open us to levels of consciousness, joy, and living that we can only glimpse right now. I believe that we are beginning to enter a revolution in these areas. This is part of the Science of the Soul that Indigo Souls carry.

7

The New Man and the New Woman

In the last section, we looked at the unfoldment of the Indigo energies in the first and second chakras. In this section, we will explore the Indigo energies as they unfold through the third and fourth chakras. As these two chakras have so much to do with the male and female within us, we will explore them in the context of the New Man and the New Woman.

The New Man

The emerging Indigo energies are creating a revolution in men. Let's begin by looking at the energies of these New Men, because the archetypes that are unfolding within men are very significant for us as individuals and for us as a race. An almost entirely new dimension of manhood is emerging. To understand this dimension, I would like to put it into the perspective of the opening of the various centers in the human energy field.

Humankind has been primarily polarized in the lower three chakras for the last many thousands of years. The energies of the lower three chakras focused and expressed via the third chakra, the chakra of power and ego. This meant that men were dominated by third chakra consciousness: competition, aggression, power, and ego. This created a self-centered and hierarchical approach to life. Men were out for themselves, and they were out to gain as much status and power for themselves as they could by climbing the ladder of hierarchy.

This is changing significantly now. The incoming Indigo energies are having a powerful impact on the heart chakra of men. The hearts of men are beginning to open in significant new ways. And additionally, the energies of the third chakra have begun to stream upwards into the heart. This means that the values of cooperation, appreciation, honor, and sensitivity are opening to a new level in men. One way we see this expressed is as respect for one another, and a willingness to cooperate rather than compete. Another way is as humanitarianism and a generosity of spirit. It is seen as an honoring of life in all its many forms, and in that honoring an unwillingness to do harm or cause pain to other living beings.

The opening of the heart is expanding our capacity for higher feelings, bringing gentleness, a subtleness of feeling, and a care, and warmth. Because of these qualities these New Men are relating to life differently. You could say that the New Men are men of 'feeling'—delicate, gentle, and deep feelings. Although there have always been some men who were heart-centered, this is new for mankind on such a widespread level. We have been dominated by the archetypes of man as strong, powerful, and domineering. Though those values still have great sway within our society, a man's value is more and more coming to be seen through the gentleness and heartfulness he carries.

Men are suffering a new type of inner tension because the heart hurts when he is egoistical

This process is not easy for men! It is bringing some very deep challenges to us. One reason is because many men who carry these new Indigo energies also carry the powerful solar plexus energies from our past. Competition is still there, egoism is still there, selfishness is still there. Now these forces are struggling with the energies of the heart that want to step beyond these things. So a great number of men are in an inner tension due to the conflict between these two centers.

In the past a man could be selfish and aggressive, and not suffer much from feelings of guilt or a bad conscience. Now that is not so. When the lower energies of the solar plexus are active our heart hurts. Often these solar plexus energies are so strong that we cannot stop them. We may be taken over by them and not even be aware of our heart in these moments, but afterwards we do become aware and our heart suffers. Many Indigo men are suffering because of the rawness of their own solar plexus. This suffering can remain for a substantial period of time until the energies polarize upwards and we come to rest in the heart center.

The second shift that is happening because of the Indigo energies stimulating the third and fourth chakras has to do with a shift to vulnerability. In the past, the definition of a man was to be strong and courageous—a hero. We should not show fear, we should not show cowardice, we should not show emotion, and we should not show pain. This image served an evolutionary purpose. Men were learning to control the fears originating from the base chakra (fear of death and pain), so that we could more intelligently respond to situations rather than only reacting instinctually with flight or fight. Though there will always be further steps we need to take in 'base chakra management', the basics of that process have been served to the extent that we can take our next steps. One component of that next step is becoming vulnerable.

The opening of our hearts and becoming vulnerable means that a man can cry, a man can admit weakness. A man can honor his needs, a man can have feelings. Being vulnerable takes an even greater courage than facing danger. Many men are willing to face physical dangers, such as going to save someone in a burning building. But how many men are willing to admit that they are frightened, to open to their needs, to let their tears come when they are hurt? Very few men are willing to take that challenge. But this is what the Indigo energies are opening in us.

In a sense, the greatest challenge that an Indigo man can embrace is his own femininity and vulnerability. This doesn't mean that he becomes powerless, a victim, or effeminate. It means he has the courage to be vulnerable, to be in his feelings, and in particular, he has the courage to love. What we see in inner work is that to open oneself to intimacy and love is perhaps the greatest challenge that exists. We do love but we tend to love from behind a wall. We stay safe. We love from a role, perhaps the protector, or provider, or caretaker. But this is a type of love without deep intimacy. Intimacy means one opens, one drops one's walls, one can be touched. The essence of the other, and the essence of you, meets. This is a delicate state, a gentle state. In it you are vulnerable, because you can be hurt. This is the challenge that Indigo men are being asked to embrace: to become vulnerable and open in love.

The new archetypes of power in men

Another significant shift that is occurring as the heart center in men opens is a putting of one's ego to the side and shifting from 'me' to 'we.' In the past we were deeply wrapped in ego. We men lived for self-centered reasons. We are now beginning to recognize our interrelationship and our connectedness to others, and that what happens to others happens to us because we are all connected. Because of this awareness of connectedness we are learning to think more in terms of the whole, and supporting the good of the whole.

This can be summed up in the often heard expression 'the sense of community,' or, using a more esoteric expression, 'group consciousness.' We are learning to open to a sense of community and the wider group life that we are part of. We are coming to see ourselves as cells within the larger body of the whole. What is good for the whole is fundamentally what is good for us. Power becomes separated from the ego. You can say that what is unfolding is the 'power of love,' versus the 'love of power,' the 'power to do good' versus 'power for power's sake.'

This is a very big step because we are learning to put aside our self-importance, to put aside our ego. We are learning to open to others, to become receptive to others, and not hold to our way as the truth and the only truth. We are learning to cooperate instead of compete.

As the ego gets put aside, there arises another aspect from the higher octave of the third chakra that has great importance for us: the sense of individuality. Individuality has become one of the highest values in the world today. People of all nations and all cultures seek to be themselves, to find their own unique form of expression. People want to make their own way. This type of individuality is new for men. In the past we did not know individuality as much as we knew ego. The archetypal structure of the world was based on those whose egos were the loudest and could grab the most power.

This is bringing a unique challenge to men. The challenge is: "What do I do with my individuality?" "Who am I really?" "What do I really want?" "What shall I make of my life?" "What is really me versus my ego?" We are being challenged to listen inwards. We are being challenged to discover what our authentic self is, and what does it mean to live authentically.

In the past what we called our individuality was, to a great extent, the self-centered narcissism of the child in us and the ego. As selfish children we did what we wanted. We didn't care so much about the repercussions to others, we just cared that we got what we wanted, that we were number one, and that it served our momentary pleasure. Now this is changing. It has to change! As a race we have more power today than we have ever had: whether it is the power of a large car or a big machine, corporate or financial power, the power to change the Earth, the power to affect the human body, the power of the mind…We have immense powers. We cannot let the self-centered ego use these powers for its own purposes. There is just too much at risk.

Many of the ways we are suffering on our planet are due to our irresponsible and selfish misuse of power. Many of the problems that we face today such as over-population, pollution, environmental damage, war, terrorism, and many others are the direct result that we have not come into the respect and responsibility that is needed. As New Men, we have new strengths, sensitivities, and responsibilities. We have to embrace those responsibilities and mature the self-centered child within into a wise adult.

To balance this power we must now, more than ever, be responsible for the effects of this power on the interrelated whole of life. It requires us to find a new definition and sense of our individuality that is in accord with our higher nature, our heart, our vision, and a higher purpose. This new definition of individuality would integrate the opposites of standing solidly in yourself as a unique and empowered human being, and being able to put your ego to the side and work together within a group for the highest good. This will bring forth the greatest power and the greatest good.

The New Woman

Women are entering into their power, responsibility, and respect

I would like to talk about Indigo women. There is a new archetype and energy unfolding in woman. Women have essentially been enslaved for thousands of years. This is now changing. For the first time women are entering equality with men. Women are entering into their power, into a new responsibility, into a new respect. This is coming about because the third chakra (power) and the fourth chakra (heart) together are forming a new integration and unit in the human psyche for both men and women.

We saw that in men the third chakra had been very active and the fourth had been more closed. In women the heart was very active but the third chakra, the power center, was somewhat collapsed or limited. Women were heartful, but they didn't have their power. They were open and generous, but oftentimes lacked the connection to their own individuality. And the power that women did have was generally lived within tight parameters. In the last 30-50 years, we have seen this change significantly. The women's liberation movement was an external reflection of the opening of the solar plexus in women.

Women are learning what it means to come into their power. It is not an easy task. Your tendency is to keep yourself small, to give your power away, to not stand for yourself. This has lead to much suffering for you. One of the ways this happens is that you give yourself away and then get taken advantage of. Part of your learning is to confront the energy pattern in yourself of the victim. In the past you were often in the victim role. Because there was really very little you could do about it, though you suffered, there was also a certain level of acceptance or resignation.

That is not the case for you today. If you give your power away, or you are collapsed by someone else, you are in pain, and it makes you sad, depressed, angry, or bitter. The emerging strength of your solar plexus is making you want to break out of the box of victimhood. You have to break out, you cannot stay small! The problem is, you don't know yet how to be big. So the challenge for women is to be big, have space, take space, have presence, be wide, be potent, be direct and strong and out there. This doesn't mean that you lose the quality of your heart; it means you can trust these qualities now to guide your power.

The New Woman: Setting the standard for a new type of relating and relationship

As this new opening occurs in you, you are setting a standard for a new type of relating and relationship. We can call it 'depth relating.' You are demanding from the men in your life a new level of connection and intimacy based on meaning and authenticity. You want and need presence: you need a man to be there and meet you—with his feelings. You are not satisfied to be in traditional roles: woman only as wife, as a mother, even as a romantic partner.

You expect a level of openness and intimacy, depth and communication. You are willing to open yourself in vulnerability and you need your man to open himself in vulnerability. Because of this you have become very challenging to the men! I want to say to you that it is part of your task as women to educate the men in your life. Men are opening to their hearts, but it is still an effort and a struggle. Of course there are always new steps of openness that can happen for you too, but in many respects your heart is already open in some significant ways. Part of your learning as woman is to find the self-respect and strength and honor to become a leader and step into the role of guiding men into love.

There are many subtle and fine energies easily accessible to you. The energies and vibrations in men tend to be more course and rough. Even for us men who are willing to open, it is a hard and difficult job. We have to shift our vibrational state from a lower vibration to a higher vibration. This can be almost physically painful for us, and we need support and guidance to do it. So women, you are being challenged by life to honor and take responsibility for the fine energies that you hold, and to let these energies become more dynamic and active. The men in your life are wanting it, and needing it, and although they will resist and they will squawk, underneath they are open to it, and it is your job to trust that and to take the initiative.

On a deeper level, if you look at the problems in the world today, they are primarily caused by men: wars, crimes, raping of the land, and so much more are fundamentally male issues. The qualities that you hold as women are needed desperately. If your solar plexus does not come into action, then you remain a victim of men and of the past, and these beautiful qualities that you have remain ineffective. Women, it is essential that you awaken your solar plexus, your power, and that you integrate it with your heart and then act from it. Your men need it. The world needs it.

We have more power than we have ever had before, but our maturity has not caught up with our power. As women you have a respect for life, you have a willingness to put yourself aside and to give to the greater good, and you have a deep sense of community. We men in the world need to be taught by you. I want to lay a challenge before you: that in many ways the future rests with you, because it is within you that the new values of the new humanity are so present and expressed. Us men, we are growing, but not fast enough compared with the powers that we have gained and the world's needs. You women already have a maturity, awareness, and heartfulness. Awaken to your strength, take your responsibility.

The New Woman expects a level of honesty in relationship that was almost unheard of in the past

This brings up the theme of expression. A new type of relating based on depth and communication is emerging. You want to speak about real things, real feelings. You are not satisfied to remain on the surface in your communications. And you expect in your relationships a level of honesty that is almost unheard of in the past. This honesty is not easy. Oftentimes it means revealing what one would rather not reveal about oneself: one's vulnerabilities, one's imperfections, or one's shame. And it often means putting the mirror of awareness up before the other, so the other can see those same types of things in themselves. So women, as you are opening to your strength, you are also opening to a new level of communication that is both a challenge and a gift. You are expecting a relationship based on truth and not lies, honesty and not deceptions, directness versus indirectness. This is summed up very well in the statement I mentioned earlier that I'd like to repeat again now. Buddha said:

> *"A lie is sweet in the beginning, but bitter in the end.*
> *Truth is bitter in the beginning, but sweet in the end."*

This simple statement sums up one of the fundamental shifts that the Indigo Energies are bringing: relationships based on truth. In our next talk, we will look at this in more detail.

Questions & Answers

• *(From a man) I see that I am mostly acting out of my solar plexus. This is where I feel the most concentration of energy. When I feel that strong energy here, my heart is almost completely closed and disconnected. And yet, I aspire to all these ideals of communication, connection, and intimacy you spoke about.*

You mentioned earlier that you work in construction. That is a solar plexus environment. And yet you are a man with a lot of heart, an opening heart. How is it for you to be in that world?

Challenging! And contradictory. It was good for me to go into it. It was good to discover my male energy, and I really enjoyed being in it. One part of me feels at home there. But I also chose to go into that work as a rebellion against my parents who wanted me to be successful in 'their' way, and now I feel kind of stuck there. And on the other side, I am very heartful but almost too heartful, too feminine with my partner. I don't live my strength there with her so much. I can't find a balance between my male construction worker and my heartfulness.

You are reminding me of something I mentioned earlier, something that is happening to many men. There are many men who have swung to the opposite side of the pendulum. As the heart is opening, they disengage and disconnect from the strength of the solar plexus, or they compartmentalize and live one in one area and one in another area, but not in a balance and integration. The challenge is to keep your already open heart present simultaneously with your solar plexus. You need its strength and solidity and dynamism in balance with the heart. This is a big job. It is not easy to integrate these two centers together. And you might be surprised: even though you are with a New Age woman she still needs a bit of your macho, your manliness. The heartful part of us thinks, "Oh no, my woman only wants a spiritual, loving, sensitive man." But my experience is that even the most spiritual of women wants and needs a man who is solid in his power.

• *(A woman) I am really enjoying this talk today because it is making many things very clear to me. I have been in this process myself, of shifting from the heart to the solar plexus, and trying to integrate them. But I also have a lot of resistance to it, and it's causing me a really hard time. From what you are saying, I can see that it is not only me that is going through this difficulty, but so many others also. And also what you describe about what a woman wishes from her man, it is something I can relate to because I also feel this.*

What is the resistance you are having with your solar plexus?

I have an idea in my head, so to speak, that power and force are something bad.

There is an old idea that spirituality is against power. A spiritual person is gentle and soft. I would like to support a new understanding, that spirituality is as much about power as it is about love and consciousness. Spirituality is an opening to the soul and the higher dimensions of what we are. The soul is an immense entity. The potency that you carry, the range of energies, and the power of those energies is tremendous. Spiritual growth is an opening to greater and greater dimensions of the powers and capacities of the soul. In a sense spirituality is learning to use constructively, creatively, and respectfully, these powers. We use an expression in inner work. We say that the soul is composed of three streams of energy—power, love, and intelligence—and that these three link together to form one purpose—creatorship.

We say that the fundamental purpose of the soul is to use power, motivated by love and guided by intelligence, for the purpose of creative and conscious living.

And these three woven together become creativity. The soul is essentially a creative entity. The soul is a creator learning creatorship.

In a way what you are saying feels like the solution to peace. The woman is love and she needs to connect with her power, and the man is power needing to connect with his love.

I think that this is probably one of the most fundamental tasks facing all of us today. This integration of power and love are one of our most central learnings. In a way a lot of the planet's evolution depends on men integrating their female side, women integrating their male side, and men and women integrating with each other.

• *In your talk you really gave a challenge to women in a very direct way. If you would have to say the same to men, like, "Men, I would challenge you to...," what would the message be?*

First, to elevate, empower, and honor women. We really only know how to be on top or to be little children with them. By coming into our hearts and by stepping out of our old solar plexus patterns, and then integrating the two, we are learning to pull our egos back and to let the woman shine, to support the woman to come into her power and her dynamism.

Second, your challenge is to become heart-centered: to open to feelings, to open to vulnerability, and to talk about them.

And third, I could say to men: "Think of the greater good, not just your own personal good. Recognize that there is a greater life that is happening. You don't need to be number one and so egotistical all the time. Learn to cooperate and work together."

I think that many men are using that. They are proving how great they are through showing off how much they are thinking of the greater good.

Our heart *is* opening and we are genuinely doing some very generous, altruistic, and heartful things. But our solar plexus is still very much present, and it remains involved with even our purer feelings or actions. We are touching here on a male core wound. The wound that we are not enough is so strong that we *have* to prove how good we are. So even though our hearts are coming in, it will take a while for that wound to heal.

I feel that women are also responsible for the situation by not coming into their power and by instinctually wanting the men to be big and powerful. I feel this is part of the dilemma of the New Age woman: she wants to come into her power, and she wants equality, but her instincts want her man to be the macho guy, because that makes her feel safe. I feel like there is a war within ourselves between our consciousness and our instincts.

The challenge for women is that your higher consciousness wants a gentle and sensitive man, but your instinctual patterns want a man with a powerful solar plexus. There are not many men around yet who have both. The challenge for most men is to become vulnerable. I think men deep down are very vulnerable, but it completely freaks out our solar plexus which needs to maintain the illusion that it is strong. Behind all our masks and our puffed up solar plexus lie shame and vulnerability. But our instincts freak out about facing this. Our instincts say, "If you are vulnerable then you are weak and not a man, and then you will loose and you are a dead-end." So we would rather almost die than reveal these feelings.

And then there are many men who have shifted to the heart, but in the process their solar plexus has diminished in an unbalanced way and they are too soft, lacking strength, not in their power. They have heart but they also have strong belly energies, the energies of the child. For women, there is an attraction to this type of man, because these men can be more intimate and meet you in the more subtle spaces, and something in your mother instincts reaches out to the vulnerable inner child within them. But at the same time, these men usually don't have the power and strength that you need, and you don't want to care-take a man who is a lot in his child. You want a man with some power! Your instincts want a man who makes you feel safe, secure, provided for. But these powerful men usually don't have the openness of the heart. And with these powerful men you again give away your power. What a headache! How to get both?

That is the learning: to develop a balance of the vulnerability with strength. So men, your challenge is to open your vulnerability and feelings, and still keep your strength. And women, it is to open to your power while keeping contact with your love. This is a process of shifting from instinct to consciousness. In consciousness you can have them both at the same time.

• *I was wondering, is it easier for men to come into their heart with all their strength and power, or for women to come into her power and strength from her heart.*

I think that they are both difficult and I don't know if it would be fair to say that one is more difficult than the other. But if I were to be really honest, when I look around our planet I see women becoming empowered and stepping into their power everywhere, and I see a much smaller number of men stepping into their hearts and vulnerability with strength. So I suspect it may be more difficult for men. I could even go a step further with this and say that woman already have their power, but they have been conditioned to feel they don't have it.

I see so many women already living their power. Whether it is in the professional sense, or as a woman alone and bringing up children, providing for her family, and the power she has to manage all this. Women are generally more integrated, their power is available, and they already have a higher sense of values and a higher consciousness. Women just need to now take in their hands their capacities and their strengths and put them into action, and to overcome their fear to challenge men because of our aggression.

• *I just find it so important, so essential, that this information becomes public and available to all men and women so that they can understand what is happening and really go through this maturing process in a productive way.*

It is very important and so many women are quite open to it, but the men are quite resistant to it. It is obvious to women how much they have to gain: they come out of being small, they get their power, etc. For men, all we see is that we are giving up something that we have been fighting to get. Why should we give up when we don't really see the gain on the other side?

Because it feels better.

The problem is that we're not so in touch yet with our feelings, so we don't know that it feels better!

• *(A man) I can really feel that. It is one thing to be vulnerable and open, but as soon as I get hurt, I cut off immediately. It is so difficult for me to really stay in my feelings. Even though the knowledge and experience is there that it does feel better, I immediately go back into my normal and more powerful role. And then I almost forget that the feeling space ever existed.*

• *(A man) I think the key to be able to stay vulnerable is that you need to learn certain tools that will help you to stay vulnerable in a painful situation. This is a crucial point. Without those tools we men will not be able to stay in vulnerability.*

• *(A woman) In nature, for men to be vulnerable means you are going to get killed. So if we women can understand this, we can work with the men. The problem for us women is that we have been so long dominated that we want revenge and want to bring you down. What often happens is that when we women come into our power then we kick the men out of revenge.*

Well, it looks like we have a lot of work ahead of us! What I see all over the world is that the attendance of growth-oriented workshops averages around 80 percent women and 20 percent men. We've got a great pool of women maturing rapidly. And then on top of that a lot of women are going for their careers and in other ways coming into their power. So we have in the world a growing imbalance. There are many more women who are becoming spiritually mature than there are men. It is for this reason that I suspect that women will become one of the dominant forces in the world for helping us take the next step.

8

The Unfoldment of Indigo Souls through the Upper Chakras

The Fifth Chakra

Our Soul has a Song to Sing

One of the deepest urges of Indigo Souls is to speak and express oneself. It is as if there is a great force erupting inside of us that wants to come out. This comes out through the throat chakra, the chakra of expression and communication. The theme of the throat chakra is summed up in one of the foundational statements of the American Constitution:

'The Freedom of Speech'

I'm not a historian, but as I remember, this may be the first time in history that freedom of speech has become law and the foundation of a nation. Up until that time we did not have freedom of speech. If you spoke things that were not accepted, or not popular, or against the status quo, you endangered yourself. Now a nation is recognizing that every person should be safe to speak their truth. But because it is written in the constitution doesn't mean that it is a reality.

These visionary types of ideas come in from the higher dimensions of existence. As they penetrate the human sphere of thinking, they become 'ideals' that we aspire towards. So the idea of freedom of speech has become an 'ideal' of freedom of speech that is gradually penetrating into our psyches. Though we certainly have more freedom today than we have ever had before, each one of us still has to learn to live this ideal and speak our truth. That is because thousands of years of persecution still sit in our minds, in our bodies, and in our collective psyche. These fears of persecution sit as deep tensions in our body and in particular around our throat. They act as a brake, inhibiting our expression.

Most of us have major blocks in our throat chakra because of these fears. This results in us holding back on speaking our deeper truths. These truths might be sharing our visions and dreams, aspirations and joys, or they might be confronting destructive behaviors and patterns in the world around us.

As an Indigo, you see a great deal. The developments in your third eye which we spoke about earlier help you perceive more deeply into what is going on in situations. And there are a lot of hidden shadow energies at play. You see the injustices, ignorance, manipulations, power games, and ego trips. You see the way people are exploited, how selfish interests do damage to the ecology, how politicians deceive people, how religions create hypnosis, and so much more. And on a more personal level you see things that are off with the people with whom we relate: the ego, greed, power, illusions, fears, wounds, and so many other things.

What you are seeing is not just fantasies of your mind—you ARE seeing. So what are you supposed to do with what you see? Well, it's part of our job as Indigos to help clean up the mess that our planet is in. And one of the ways you can do this is by talking about it.

You are being challenged to move into a higher level of honesty than you might be used to. You are learning to talk about the difficult things. There is a very narrow bandwidth of things that we normally talk about. These are the 'acceptable' things, the safe things. Outside that bandwidth things become more difficult and challenging—perhaps revealing something about yourself that you normally hide, or not saying something to somebody because of how they might react. For many reasons we mute things that we would like to express.

You have to work through your inhibitions and fears of communicating and come out. It is a big jump to reveal and express your self. There is always a moment of fear in doing it. In the beginning it may create awkward moments, or tensions, or reactions. And many of the things that you would like to talk about will not be so well received; at least in the beginning, though it is worth it in the end.

You have to 'rock the boat.' And though there are some Indigo Souls who are the crusader type and do this more regularly, (you are learning the art of doing it skillfully, not with a sledgehammer), most Indigo Souls are essentially heart-based and gentle and don't want to do something that will hurt another person. Because of that you will often swallow your words, swallow your truth. You are afraid that if you say your truth to another, they will not be able to take it and will be hurt.

Well, the truth is that as an Indigo Soul you *are* going to stir people up. You are going to shake them, upset them, and challenge them. You are doing it just by being you. You don't even have to say anything. There is something different in your energy. And the more you begin to speak up, there is a good chance that people will react against you more vehemently: they may get defensive, or angry, or they may attack you. They may put up a wall against you, or they may pull away from you.

And yet you really have no choice but to be in the truth and deal with the consequences, because if you compromise yourself or don't live in your authenticity the suffering is even worse. It is not easy for you to be false. You cannot easily play games or sell yourself short. Being in integrity is a powerful force within you. This will challenge you to speak and express your truth at a more risky level than your environment or your own internal safety mechanisms would like.

And perhaps the ultimate risk, even larger than speaking about the so-called 'negative' things, is to speak about the positive. At the deepest level there is something of our Essence, a song, as if our soul has a song to sing. There is so much beauty and magic that we sense and see, there are so many moments of joy that we would like to share. So much we would like to create. So to sing one's song means to express that which is the closest, most intimate within ourselves.

There is a good example that we all know concerning the challenge to do this. Let's say you've had a bad day. Imagine going into your work environment and talking about this. Probably not too difficult. Most of us are pretty much used to griping about things. Now imagine the opposite: you've had an incredible moment, something that moved you so much. Imagine being in your work environment and saying to people: "I had such an incredible experience. I feel like my heart opened thiiiiisssss much. It's as wide as a house. I feel just this universal love and compassion and joy in me." Not so easy to do, is it? It's as if there is a taboo against speaking too much of the positive, too much of the beauty that we experience. And yet, wouldn't it be great if we could? If you listen to some of the mystic poets, such as Rumi or Tagore or Whitman, it's just this that makes their poetry so beautiful and attractive. Why can't we do it too?

To sing one's song means to be living your life in alignment with your soul, with your Essence. Your life becomes an expression and a testament of what you stand for: your highest ideals and aspirations, your beliefs and commitments, your joy and ecstasy.

Changing the world through the creative energies of the throat

The world is built upon energetic thought forms and patterns. Many of these thought forms are ancient, going back thousands of years. They are deeply entrenched, limiting life, and not letting the spirit flow. Part of your job as an

Indigo Soul is to help break up these old thought and energetic structures and create new energetic forms. Your throat is a powerful creative tool to do this. In some ways the throat is the most powerful emitter of energy streams in the body. The streams that it sends out are not only words, they are also vibrations. These words and vibrations are powerful forces that break up old structures and create new ones.

To do this you are learning to use your thoughts and words in a more deliberate process. We call this process 'creatorship.' Your throat emits vibrations that affect and sculpt the world around you. That is why it is called the creative chakra. What we call fifth chakra consciousness is the awakening to your self as a creator. In that sense Indigo Souls are some of the most creative people ever. If you look at society since the turn of the century, we have created more in this last 100 years than perhaps has ever existed previously on the planet. We have created scientifically and medically, in the arts and music, and we have created architecture, cities, genetics, farming...The list goes on and on. In the last one hundred years we have seen an explosion of the creative spirit on this planet. This is a result of the incoming Indigo energies. And this is just the beginning. We are right now developing tools: computers, Internet, communication media, satellites, and so much more, that will be tremendous assets to opening the creative expression of humanity.

So I would like to say to you: "Find your creativity," whatever form it's meant to take. Find it because it is needed. Find it because it's part of your destiny to be a creator at greater and greater levels.

Perhaps your creativity will express through being an artist or a scientist. But you can be just as creative in your kitchen, on your computer, talking with your friend, sweeping your floor. The spirit in you is vast and potent, and it wants to create. You are a visionary. You are the sculptor of a planet. You hold a blueprint of a new type of human being and a whole new type of living. That creation is taking place inside of you. Ultimately your creation is going to be the creation of yourself. You are meant to create yourself into that ideal. And then you are meant to create your life as an embodiment of that ideal—your every interaction with people and situations can carry that energy. I want to say to you, "Take the challenge, and create the life that you sense you were created to live." At this moment in time, the door is open. This is a very special moment in history, where immense vital and creative forces are available, where there is an openness in humanity, where we can create a life that is magnificent.

The Unfoldment of the Sixth Chakra

The theme of creativity leads me to the unfoldment of energies in the sixth chakra. Much of the earlier material in this book is about the sixth chakra as this chakra is so central to Indigo Souls. We've already spoken of the opening of the third eye and the new aspects of consciousness that are unfolding. We've looked at the visionary and idealistic aspects of Indigo consciousness, and we've explored the development of the mind, as well as the 'ideals of the new' that Indigos carry and are seeking to manifest.

I'd like to look now at the workings of the third eye and its relationship to the crown chakra and soul consciousness. The upper third eye is connected to the crown chakra, and to an eighth chakra, about 12 inches above the head, called the Higher Self, or sometimes called the seat of the soul. These three centers begin to work as an integrated unit. We call this 'The Light in the Head.'

What this means is that the soul, carrying a very high level of intelligence, insight and understanding, begins to stream these energies downwards via the crown chakra and into the third eye. We experience them as moments of insight, clarity, or inspiration. These are the transcendent moments we sometimes touch in meditation, or sometimes we touch them for no apparent reason. Whatever the case, for a moment it is as if a veil is withdrawn and you have a moment of clarity and insight. The plane of the soul has penetrated into waking consciousness via the third eye.

This process occurs through a channel between the soul, the crown, and the third eye, called the rainbow bridge, or in Sanskrit, the Antahkarana. The Antahkarana is substantially developed in Indigos, giving them a lot of access to soul consciousness. This consciousness comes through in a couple of ways; either as 'intuitive knowing,' or as clarity of mind. Both ways think outside the box, meaning your thinking is not conditioned by the usual way things have been.

These two aspects of the third eye create two distinct types of Indigo Souls. The intuitive types have a dominant right brain (non-linear thinking) and upper third eye. These people work more through intuition and get a lot of their information from 'gut feelings,' or the 'little voice inside.' They exhibit an unusual level of intuitional or psychic development.

The left-brain dominant types are more connected to the lower third eye (analytic mind) and have a clear, sharp, and penetrating logic. It gives them an unusual level of mental development and clarity. These people are the thinkers, the great minds.

Most Indigos are polarized on one side or the other, some being more the mental types, and others being the more intuitive type. Occasionally you get someone who is active on both sides simultaneously. These people have direct experience into energy and the subtle world and are able to speak about it and explain it via logic and the mind.

Challenges Arising From the Third Eye

This level of activity in the third eye is not without its challenges, because the opening of the third eye brings a very high frequency of energy. These energies move very fast, they jump around, and they literally have the quality of electricity. In astrology electricity is ruled by the sign Aquarius. It was only as the Indigo energies came in as we began entering the Age of Aquarius that we discovered electricity. Electricity has now become a dominant force on the planet. There is almost nowhere that you can go on the planet today where you are not inundated with a bombardment of electrical frequencies. Whether it is emissions from the electrical wiring in a house or a building, the wires in the streets, the electrical frequencies of cell phones, television, and satellites, we are being inundated with a field of electrical energy that didn't exist one hundred years before.

This electrical field is connected to an expansion of intelligence. Look at its expressions: electricity is used in machines that we have developed to make our life easier. We use electricity in lights so we can see in the dark; we use electricity in telecommunications and computers. It is through electricity that vast amounts of information are moving on the planet. The information age would not exist if it were not for electricity. And both the proliferation of electricity and the proliferation of information are a reflection of the opening of the intelligence in the third eye.

Now this is a great step. We are evolving rapidly. But along with this evolution come many challenges. These are primarily two-fold. The first is that the mind has not been developed to handle this massive amount of information. Most of us are in information overload. All this information is going into our minds and through our mind into the nervous system and to our entire body. The result is that nervous disorders are tremendously enhanced by the Indigo energies: restlessness, ulcers, inability to sleep, skin problems, or the many other difficulties that arise on the physical level because of the heightened activity of the nervous system. It is because of this that it is essential for Indigo Souls to ground: to ground the body, to use it, to keep it vital, to bring the energy through it and to the Earth.

The second challenge that we see with these energies is connected with what doctors have called A.D.D., attention deficit disorder. Many Indigo Souls, especially the younger ones who have come in more recently, their minds are too fast for the normal school or work system. On the one hand, this says something about the system, it has not adapted to these new souls. Our schools are challenged to find new methods of educating these new children, and the work environments of putting their intelligence to use.

But a big part of the issue also lies with the Indigo Souls themselves. As new energies and frequencies come in, they stimulate developments and flows within the human energy system that the system itself is not yet used to handling. Many of the problems that you are dealing with are because your nervous system is having too much amperage, too much voltage flowing through it. Gradually, overtime our system will adapt. We will be able to handle the Indigo frequencies more easily. Right now this is a problem for many people, and we need to find temporary solutions to help handle the energy until our system is strong enough.

The development of the mind has outpaced the development of the emotions and the body

Another challenge for Indigo Souls that results from the new activities within the third eye is that the development of the mind has outpaced the development of the emotions and of the body. This is typified in the archetype of the 'computer nerd.' These people are exemplified either by a guy with a smart-looking head and either a skinny body, kind of dangling beneath it that is over-amped and ungrounded, or the opposite, a blobby, out-of-shape body housing a very intelligent mind.

These types of people are part of the new breed of people on the planet, people in whom the mind is so highly developed but in a way that is not much connected to the body. These people don't live in the body. This is not in balance. But we need to be balanced to be healthy. Imbalance leads to ill health, both psychologically and physically. What we see from an evolutionary perspective is that evolution often swings between polarities as it progresses. Now we're swinging to a new polarity very quickly, but it will take a while for the whole system to catch up and adjust.

This creates a problem at another level: it is a problem for women giving birth. One of the reasons that birth has become such a painful and difficult process is that the size of the cranium has grown very rapidly in terms of evolutionary time. The pelvis of a woman was not built to put such a large cranium through it. So it is creating more pain in the birth process, longer labors, and more difficult births.

The evolutionary process does not happen in a balanced and harmonious way, where everything works together. It happens where one part takes a big step but another part lags behind.

The biggest challenge is to become an 'integrated personality,' guided by the soul

So the emergence of the Indigo energies are, on the one hand, a tremendous and wondrous gift to humanity, but on the other hand they are bringing many problems. I could sum up all these challenges in one short statement: "The challenge of intelligence." Intelligence is energy and it has a vibratory frequency. We are learning to handle these tremendous new energies of intelligence. As Indigo Souls it is our task to learn about these new powers: how to handle them through our bodies and energy system, how to handle the information overload that our intelligence is creating, how to integrate this intelligence with our heart, with our emotions, with our body, with our soul, with many other parts of our selves.

One of the first steps in becoming integrated occurs through 'turning the eye upward.' To use a metaphor, imagine a flashlight. Normally we have the flashlight turned outwards to illuminate the world around. Now imagine that you turn the flashlight inward instead of outward. It begins to illuminate our psychology and the world of energy. Next turn it inward and upward, toward the crown chakra and beyond. It begins to illuminate our soul. The basic principle of energy work is, 'Energy flows where awareness goes.' By turning the eye of awareness upward it brings energy to the crown and the soul. It stimulates the opening of the Antahkarana and the connection to our higher nature. At a particular point in this process there is a radical shift in consciousness. This is the moment of awakening. You become soul-conscious.

This awakening to the soul is a momentous step in the spiritual journey. It would be so tempting to stop here. But it is not the end of the journey. A further step in this process is the bringing down of soul energies into the chakras. This creates an entirely new state of consciousness within each chakra, restructuring the chakras in a way that they hold more energy and can function in a new capacity. This stage of the process is called 'Building the Body Divine.'

It is in this stage that the soul and the personality integrate together to become a 'soul-infused personality.' In a 'soul-infused personality' spiritual purpose from the soul becomes present in the crown, where it is held as life purpose. You have a sense of knowing why you are here, and your life has a focus of meaning, direction, and purpose. Life purpose from the crown is then expressed as vision and clarity in the third eye. You are clear on what you need to do here, in this world, at this moment. Through your mind you can apply your higher purpose to clear and grounded goals.

The third eye then becomes like the conductor of the inner orchestra; it guides and aligns the many sub-personalities and chakras beneath it. In the normal state of consciousness, the chakras are like musicians in an orchestra before the conductor is present. Each is more or less doing its own thing, there is no overall guiding and integrating force. The third eye is the conductor who has the musical score given it by the crown chakra. It then begins to conduct, guiding the musicians from a cacophony into a harmony. The chakras begin to function at a higher level and serve the consciousness of the soul.

The third eye is the 'master key' for this whole process. This is because of the power of awareness that the third eye brings. Returning back to the metaphor of the flashlight, in the past 100 years we have intensified the light of the flashlight (intelligence) from 10 to 100 volts. With our powerful flashlight we have been shining the light outwards, illuminating the Universe around us (the discoveries of science). We are now beginning to shine the light of awareness inward into the inner world, opening the doors into our psychology and the world of energy. And we are just beginning now to turn the light upward to illuminate the soul and the higher world. This inward and upward turned flashlight is strong in Indigo Souls. We are recognizing a whole other dimension within and around us that has been mostly invisible to the normal mind. Indigo perception is opening a vast new panorama of intelligence, vision, energy, and spirituality—a whole other dimension of being.

Questions & Answers

• *I think we are less free than we think we are. We exist in a culture where there are very few Indigo Souls and we are strongly influenced by the past Piscean Age. There are so many limits everywhere; how can we really be free here?*

How does that sit with you?

I feel like a puppet.

There is a lot of truth in what you are saying. We are limited not only by the limits of the culture but also by many other kinds of limits: of the body, of the brain, of instincts, of gravity, of nature, of celestial sources. Many Indigo Souls are really struggling with this feeling of being limited. You don't want to be controlled by anything or anyone, whether it is politicians, society, the church, God, astrology, or the ascended masters. The Indigo energies say, "Don't mess with me."

Boy, are you in trouble! You exist here on this Earth and in this culture within immense limitation. So what are you going to do about it? Spend your entire life rebelling? I hope not. This is one of the deeper teachings of Indigo Souls: to learn to work with the limitations of the world around you. You are here to create something new, and that creative process is not easy. It's like forging a sword in a fire and hammering it to get the shape and sharpness.

Your real freedom is going to come not from fighting all the limits, or from dreaming of some idealized state which is not possible in this world. It's going to come from finding the right balance between freedom and surrender. And I want to emphasize that word—surrender. Because ultimately, as you move upward into consciousness, you learn to surrender to THAT WHICH IS. You face the paradox of total surrender and total freedom and creativity, all at the same time.

How does this sound to you?

I feel more and more compliance and indifference.

And what is underneath.

It cooks underneath. I want to escape the structures which I am in.

What I sense in you is that though you comply on the surface, underneath another part withdraws and says, "You will not get me." Is that right?

Yes.

You feel like many Indigo Souls—with a volcano boiling within you and a kind of aloof, even 'spiritual' indifference on the surface. You feel so much frustration with all the limits and stupidity you see around you and you feel helpless to do anything about it. You don't know what to do with all that frustration. So here is your challenge. And though I am speaking to you here tonight, I am speaking to the millions of Indigo Souls out there: put all that frustrated energy into dynamic creativity.

One part of you looks at the situation in the world and just rolls your eyes. You look at the kinds of people who are our political leaders. You look at what the vested power interests are doing. You look at what goes on in the name of religion. We seem so small in the face of such large powers out there that we just feel helpless, and then a part of us just turns away. That part says, "I can't make any difference, I am too small, so I will just stay in my corner and be above it." I want to say to all Indigo Souls, "Come out of your corners, become agents of social change, get involved, change your life, embody your beliefs, make waves, have fun doing it, and add your piece towards creating a world that we are all proud to live in."

• *When you talk about Indigo Souls, I think: "Oh, that is me." And it's a wonder that this involves everybody else, the whole world, it is not just me. When I am at home I think that it is just to me that these things are happening, but it is everywhere.*

You know, that reminds me of a beautiful image. Imagine you have a table, with a lot of little uncooked beans on the table, and all the beans are sitting very quietly, and then someone starts shaking the table, and all the beans start vibrating. They are all vibrating at a similar rate because it is the movement of the table that is shaking them all simultaneously. But because each bean's perspective is limited, each thinks: "Wow, how strange, I am vibrating and shaking around like this. What is with me? I am so different." Gradually as your awareness expands you see that the table is shaking, that the whole field of all the beans is shaking.

That perception is part of the opening of the upper third eye. One of the things that the third eye brings is a panoramic perspective. You see a larger whole, you see yourself interconnected as part of this whole. In a certain way, Indigo Consciousness represents a dissolving of the personal ego-centric self. You begin to recognize yourself as a cell in this vast living entity called the Earth, and within an even vaster entity called the Universe.

How is it for you when you go home and start seeing that it is not just you?

It gives me courage to come into contact with people. Because I feel that he or she also belongs to that.

That's great that you say that, because many Indigo Souls feel like they are strangers and weirdoes; you don't fit. So many Indigo Souls then isolate themselves and stay separate. Many develop an inferiority complex.

I had that, but no more.

What changed it?

Inner work.

You started to recognize yourself. And that is what is essential for Indigo Souls. It is essential for you to do inner work. There is a paradox: although everyone needs inner work, the souls that don't have Indigo energy don't need it as much, even though they need it more. What I mean is that on certain levels they can't use a lot of the inner work that is available because a lot of the emerging new forms of inner work are more suited for Indigo Souls. It doesn't work effectively for Piscean Souls, it doesn't fit to them.

So I should not expect so much from the ones that don't open?

Exactly. Relax your expectations. Inner work is not for all people. Leave them in peace. They are evolving according to their inner timing.

Indigo Souls are coming into the body with different 'equipment.' That means certain petals of certain chakras are more active. Therefore you perceive differently, you think differently, you respond differently. Something would be ABC and so obvious to you, and you can't believe that somebody else doesn't think and see it that way.

There are many areas of the psyche where this is true, but one in particular is directly connected to the third eye. The normal state of the third eye, not the Indigo state, looks outwards. These people have a tremendous difficulty in self-reflection. Some of you will remember this example that I used before, but let me refer back to it and then elaborate upon it. If I were to ask to someone like this, "What are you feeling right now?" they might say, "Nothing special, everything is fine," even though I can look at them and see that their leg is suddenly shaking vehemently and that they are disturbed, that something is going on. Yet they don't even notice it because their focus is outwards. Indigo Souls have certain developments in the third eye which allow them to look back on themselves. You can 'self-reflect,' you can look into your self.

It is this self-reflection that allows you to be able to work on your self. I found this whole thing very strange in the beginning. I would say to someone, "Do you feel something is going on in you?" and they would say, "What do you mean, I am fine." I realized that they weren't playing a game with me; they really didn't see. It's almost like there are two different breeds of human beings. We all seem similar on the surface, so we think we are all more or less the same. But don't be fooled, there are very many different energy states and types of beings that are existing here on Earth.

• *What makes one person an Indigo Soul and another person not an Indigo Soul? How do these differences come about?*

I can answer it on a more peripheral level or on an esoteric level. I feel you are asking on an esoteric level, so I will answer it that way. The best metaphor is a major train station in a big city, where you have trains coming from many directions. One train comes from Italy and is full of Italians, another comes from Poland, full of Polish people. We see the same thing on a more cosmic level. The Earth is like a train station, and the trains coming in are filled with souls coming from different dimensions, different soul groups, different evolutionary streams, and different sources in the Cosmos.

So just as in the train station, a certain train comes at a certain time and has a certain scheduling; a certain group of souls have a certain scheduling as to when they are to arrive. That scheduling is based on great cosmic cycles—a kind of cosmic clock. These are cycles of astrology that slowly move and turn, opening certain gates in the Cosmos so that certain energy streams can flow. So when we talk about Indigo Souls I am referring to a cosmic picture of vast evolutionary celestial energies in motion according to these cosmic clocks.

That is what astrology has given me. When I first got into astrology, I wanted to figure out who I was, and why I feel and think the way I do. But as I started going into myself and seeing astrology, I found out that what I called 'me' was the concretization of vast forces operating through the planets and stars. Each one of us is a vortex of concretized celestial forces. I am not separate from the Universe at all, rather I am a most intricate and intimate dance of great cosmic energies.

Astrology became a doorway to mysticism because it expanded my consciousness to seeing these vast dimensions and forces of energies at work. One of the reasons why the Aquarian Age and the Indigo energies hold such fascination for me is because I see it as a ripple in the Cosmos. It is a cosmic ripple, preceded by other ripples and preceding ripples yet to come. As I begin to glimpse this larger unfolding whole, I perceive such magic and mystery, such immense forces and potentials.

• *What does it do within you when you see that these vast forces have something to do with you? Does it frighten you?*

I love it. I will give you an earthier picture. One of my sports is windsurfing. I spent several years windsurfing in Hawaii, which has very fine winds, waters, and waves. Sometimes I would be several miles out from the beach in the open ocean, dealing with these huge ocean waves and swells. I have been out in conditions as high as my sail, some 15 feet. There was always a moment of choice in which I could escape from the swell or catch the swell, or if I were closer in, I could catch the waves and ride them or avoid them. There was nothing as exciting as catching this huge force of nature and riding it. There were many moments when my fear was strong. Sometimes I would escape and sail away, but mostly I loved the feel of it.

And that is what I feel about the energies of the Cosmos; they are a wonderful ride, it is exciting, like 'surfing the cosmic wave.' I find it the most exciting and interesting thing to do. I am watching a new wave coming in, a wave that is building a whole new civilization. I am watching the structures, and governments, new ways of relating and communicating being born right now. This is exciting: it is not everyday you get to see a planetary civilization being born.

For me the fear is slowly receding, and a new excitement and interest are coming in. There is an excitement to see what is going to happen and what is going to emerge. Previously I never had the courage to speak the way I am doing right now. As you talk about these things, I have this urge to partake in them with you.

Great. I like to hear that.

I am putting voice to what is inside of all of us. Part of my job is to wake up my sleeping friends. I see it like this: a certain wave is coming in, and a whole group of souls come in on it. We are all basically the same, carrying the same energies and vision. But the incarnation process was a rough landing. As the souls were coming in, the airplane got bounced around—a lot of us got frightened, some of us got wounded and hurt. The result of this is that a lot of Indigo Souls have gone into a corner and clammed up, or have become confused or just 'fallen asleep.' Quite a few have gotten wounded and are curled in upon their wounds, or are limping and kind of in a daze.

In a sense you could say that my clamshell opened a few minutes earlier than some others'. So it is my job to walk around and knock on your clamshell and invite you to open it. One thing is clear: we all need to come out of our clamshells for us to do the job that we are here to do. The work of building a new civilization will take all of our energies working together. So it is really important that each one of you Indigo Souls comes into your self and becomes dynamic and potent. That is really what I am trying to do: to stimulate my friends and take them out of their clamshells, and then join hands and let's get creative, and do what we came here to do.

9

The Big Picture

Tonight is the Full Moon, and tonight is a special Full Moon. It is called the Wesak festival, or the Wesak Full Moon. In Tibet and India the Wesak festival is considered the primary spiritual festival of the year. What they say in Tibet is that 2500 years ago the Buddha was born, became enlightened, and died on this Full Moon—the Scorpio Full Moon. Since that time his consciousness has continued to expand. He has become one of the top members of the Spiritual Hierarchy who support the Earth. And his function at this point has to do with our Earth and our solar system and the way our solar system relates to even larger solar systems and energies out there. He is part of the energy linkage between different cosmic entities, so to speak.

In this role, he has little to do with normal human life. He doesn't interface with the human kingdom in any kind of direct way. But at the time of this Full Moon, this one Full Moon of the year, he comes closer to the sphere of human consciousness, as a link bringing those celestial energies to the Earth. The story is that at the exact moment of this Full Moon every year, 500 enlightened people gather in the Tibetan mountains to help bring him down. Esoteric tradition says that the energies available tonight at this Full Moon are the most potent of the whole year.

The Big Picture

Because of these larger energies of the Wesak festival tonight, I would like to look at the bigger picture creating what we call Indigo's. Up until now, we have looked at the details of living as an Indigo Soul. Tonight I would like to look at the larger context of why Indigo Souls exist in the first place and what you are meant to be doing here. We're going to start with an understanding of the Cosmos as given by esotericism, and then within that context look at Indigos.

This material is a summation of the foundations of esotericism and metaphysics. A lot of it is way out there and certainly not within the realm of our ordinary experience. It's kind of a spiritual mythology or cosmology that is far beyond what our mind normally perceives. Though we mentioned this earlier, let me say it again. Rather than believe or disbelieve this material, let me just put it before you as a hypothesis. Keep an open mind and see if it resonates with you.

The basis of esotericism is that there is One Great Life, or One Divine Being whose body is this vast Universe. And that this Great Being, or Great Life, is evolving. This entity that we call God is in a constant state of evolution and development. This Being itself is becoming more conscious, and is discovering and unfolding its own nature and potentials. This Being unfolds in 'seasons' or rhythms, and is composed of many types of energies.

Esotericism says that the Universe that we know is a deliberate creation of this Being to serve its intentions. Those intentions are called 'The Divine Plan,' or simply 'The Plan.' When we refer to The Plan, we are referring to as much as we can glimpse of the intentions of that Great Intelligence that has set the Universe in motion.

Although this Being is 'One Life,' essentially just one entity, it differentiates itself into many, many entities or beings. This is called the 'stepping down process,' in the sense that this one life becomes galaxies, and groupings of galaxies, which now become lives in their own right. When we look at a galaxy like the Milky Way, or we look through a telescope and see all these beautiful spiral galaxies, they are considered to be living entities. They are vast consciousnesses that are the stepped down consciousness of that One Great Life.

And those entities have many smaller entities that compose them, which are groups of stars within the galaxies. And that these groupings of stars separate down to each star—each sun in the sky is seen to be a living entity. And these then step down like in our solar system, where each planet is a cell within the entity that we call our Sun. And these planets too are living entities. Then we get to the Earth, which is again a living entity. We see human beings as cells within the body of the entity we call the Earth. And this goes on all the way to the atoms. Atoms too are considered living entities.

The basic picture given by esoterics is of this vast inter-relationship of lives. Each one of these lives has been created to manifest divine purpose, and each one of these lives embodies particular aspects of divinity. We see that the Universe is composed of one vast field of energy. It's called the etheric field of the Cosmos. And within this field, energy is continually moving and circulating. You can think of the ocean. There is just one ocean. But within the ocean there are streams of energy moving. For example, the Gulf Stream. We say that there are different streams of God, or universal streams of energy that flow through and circulate amongst all these different lives. That there is a constant circulation from small to large, from large to small, and amongst all these various entities.

If you use the analogy of the human body, blood is circulating through the veins and arteries. The blood will go to a particular organ or gland in which certain things are added or changed in the blood. Those changes are then carried to different cells that respond to those changes, and make their own changes to it, and then the blood carries on again in this never-ending process of movement and change.

When we expand this analogy to the universe, every entity—whether large or small—changes something in the universal energy. We are being fed by these energies, they form the basis of our life. As they change from their emanating sources, they affect and change us. We, in turn, are affecting that stream of energy and changing it. The energies continue from us into another aspect of the Universe, into the next organ or cell or entity, so that there is this constant circulation of changing, evolving frequencies of energy and consciousness.

The Earth is just a very small part within this bigger picture and within the Plan. We are just one very, very tiny dot, or speck of dust within it. And in terms of cosmic time and evolution, we are considered to be very young in the evolutionary scale of beings. When I say "we," I am not just referring to you or I. I am referring also to the entity of the Earth itself, that the Earth is very young. This entity is growing and learning. It learns in steps and stages. At this moment in time this entity is in the process of taking its next step in growth and evolution.

Just as a human being goes through various stages of growth, these planetary and cosmic entities also go through various phases of growth. In an earlier phase of the Earth's evolution, when the atoms and molecules that form the Earth first came together, one of the Earth's first evolutionary stages was to form the minerals. We say in esotericism that minerals are alive, and that the minerals form the first kingdom of the Earth—the mineral kingdom. The mineral kingdom carries particular frequencies and energies of the Earth, certain aspects of its consciousness. The mineral kingdom forms the first layer or body that the Earth evolved. It is the foundation upon which all the other kingdoms have evolved, and it is the basis upon which our own body is built.

I want to emphasize a point here because it's so out of our normal way of thinking: it seems that minerals are dead rocks as distinct from plants or animals which are obviously living. But though we cannot see a mineral move the way a plant or an animal might, it holds a particular consciousness, it holds particular frequencies of energy, and at its own level it is evolving and changing. At its own level, it too is partaking of these universal streams that compose the Cosmos—being changed by them and in turn changing them.

This living entity, the Earth, formed over many billions of years, as a part of its evolutionary unfoldment, that part of the body of itself that we call the mineral kingdom. Once the mineral kingdom had reached a certain stage of its development, the Earth took its next step that arose out of the mineral kingdom. The second step that the Earth took in its evolution was the plant kingdom.

I would like to backtrack for just a moment. Mostly we think of the Earth as a 'ball of matter.' But in esotericism it is said that the physical earth is the 'body' that is inhabited by a cosmic entity. A 'soul' so to speak, much more advanced than our soul is, incarnated itself into this ball of matter. Just as our physical body is the form that a soul is using, so the physical Earth is the form that a very advanced soul is using.

Not only did one entity incarnate into the form of the Earth, but that this entity brought with it a whole entourage consisting of many lesser lives to support it in this process. The name given in esotericism to this primary entity is Sanat Kumara, and its grouping of entities is what is commonly called the 'Spiritual Hierarchy.' Initially, the Spiritual Hierarchy came from sources outside of our solar system, the primary source being the star Sirius. Gradually, as various souls from earth evolved, some of them have entered the Spiritual Hierarchy, and other members of the hierarchy have moved on, away from the Earth's evolution to other evolutionary paths in the Cosmos.

Sanat Kumara and the Spiritual Hierarchy have, in essence, been 'growing' the Earth since the very beginning of the Earth's formation. We say the Earth is the creation of cosmic entities. That the formation of life on this Earth, the process that we call evolution, has been and is to this day, a guided and sculpted process initiated and held by higher intelligences according to The Plan. This view doesn't negate the normal understanding of evolution as arising from the forces of natural selection and genetic recombination. Those forces are also at work. But in addition, there is input from the inner side of life to shape the direction that evolution takes.

If we look at evolution on the Earth and the various developments that have occurred, such as the step from the mineral kingdom to the plant kingdom, these were moments when the hierarchy generated tremendous energy—shall we say, the heat needed so that the water could boil. These moments have been called the 'Great Approaches.' In these moments the Great Lives generated tremendous fields of force that came into the Earth's sphere and interacted with the structure of the Earth and with the structure of the energies around the Earth in certain ways that allowed the next evolutionary steps to happen.

The Animal and the Human Kingdoms

One Great Approach initiated the second kingdom, the plant kingdom, and then, after many millions of years, another Great Approach occurred to create the animal kingdom as a step emerging from the plant kingdom. The animal kingdom then went through many developmental phases until a third Great Approach came about in which human life was catalyzed from the animal stream that had become the monkeys. Many experiments were made at that time to catalyze the human kingdom. Not all those experiments were successful. It is said in esotericism that the chimpanzees, some of the other monkeys, and the gorillas were earlier experiments to bring about the human kingdom and the next step of consciousness.

Now, to make the picture even more complex, as the human kingdom was developed, the Spiritual Hierarchy was not unified. The hierarchy itself was composed of many streams of entities, many streams of souls coming from many difference sources with many different intentions and ideas about how this life on Earth should be developed. Perhaps the best metaphor is the one I used earlier but in a slightly different context: the main train station in a big city. You have trains coming in from many different countries. A train coming from one land carries people with that particular vibration and consciousness, those particular beliefs and attitudes. A train coming from another land carries another group of people with different vibrations, etc. At the main station you have this coming together of many different streams of entities. These souls will get off the train, do something, perhaps stay a little or a longer time, then get on another train and go somewhere else.

The foundation of esoteric thought is that the Earth is like a central train station. There are streams of entities and souls arriving into the station from many different directions, many different sources within the Cosmos. The early hierarchy in the beginning times of the Earth was a mix of different entities with different intentions and ideas. You could say that the 'waters became muddied' in that the initial intention and plan that had been set in motion was pushed and pulled in different directions according to these various entities and their intentions. Different groups of entities were involved in different experiments with different types of plants and animals on different continents. One of the reasons today we see so many very different types of living entities, different phylum, and also different races of human beings is not just because of evolutionary adaptations, but because of different celestial energies that were involved in creating or shaping those evolutionary streams.

Not only were these streams different, but there were also tensions and conflicts at the hierarchical level. The Earth became divided into many zones of tension and contention between different entities and different sources within the Cosmos. So when the human kingdom was created, it was created in a moment of a Great Approach where many Beings were involved, in a moment of tension amongst these creating sources.

Gradually over millions and millions of years, all of these entities and forces together, in conjunction with the 'normal' evolutionary processes, were at work to shape, evolve, and refine the human body, nervous system and brain, emotional system and mind. The purpose of this vehicle was for these incarnating spirits to have a richer vehicle to experience through. And so it is. Gradually, over these millions of years, the human system has allowed more and more of the vast consciousness of the soul to operate through it. What was once a primitive and limited vehicle for soul experience has refined and developed, allowing the soul a richer experience of this dimension, and allowing more of the soul to come through it.

When seen from a human perspective, we have come a very long way on the evolutionary journey. But when seen from a cosmic perspective, the human vehicle is still very young and primitive. Only a small amount of the soul's energy and consciousness can come through it. Evolutionary time is vast. A few million years is just a few moments in the long life of the soul. So the human vehicle that our souls exist in is still an 'early model,' an unfinished product. Not only is it unfinished, but in terms of the energies of the soul, the energies that the vehicle can carry are still very limited. Putting this in the perspective of cosmic time, we have just emerged from the jungles and forest of Earth. We have just begun to stand on two legs, to think, to develop the mind. The vehicle is still to a great degree run by the instincts that were needed in the difficult struggle for survival in Earth's jungles and forests and oceans.

Not only is the human vehicle young and relatively primitive, but it is also composed of many different streams of energy that were coming from these various sources in which the 'creating souls' originated. To use a metaphor, it is as though I were building a car, and I got one part from Japan, another part from Germany, another part from Russia, and I put them all altogether. The human form is seen to be a compilation of many parts built on many streams, with different conflicting energies, and many different non-integrated forces.

Even though the human vehicle is a little discombobulated due to these many energies operating within it, it has reached a special point in its development. Coming back to the bigger picture, the Earth as an evolving entity has developed four kingdoms: the mineral, plant, animal, and human. The human kingdom has now reached a point in its evolution where a next step can happen through it—a next step for the living entity of the Earth itself. We say that the Earth is evolving its next kingdom.

This next kingdom is referred to as the fifth kingdom, or the kingdom of souls. What this means is that for the first time these many souls that have been a part of the inner dimension of the life of the Earth, can incarnate and *retain the full consciousness of themselves as souls.* Previous to this time, when a soul would incarnate into the human vehicle, due to the limitations of the human vehicle only a fragment of the soul's consciousness could be embodied. Though the soul was the indwelling and animating life of the body, the majority of the consciousness of the soul remained outside of and disconnected from the body, the personality, and the mind. To a great extent, this 'vehicle' of the body/personality ran primarily on instinctual-bio-computer programs that had been built up over millions and millions of years of evolution.

Let me use an example to help explain this. Most of you have had what are commonly called 'spiritual experiences': moments of a wider consciousness, moments of connection to 'something higher.' Perhaps you call it your higher self, your soul, the masters or angels, your guides, or God. For a moment your consciousness was elevated into another level. And then you lost it again. When you were in that consciousness you saw the world differently, you felt differently, and you might have acted differently. You became a different person from who you normally are.

What happened is that for a moment you went beyond the limited consciousness of the human vehicle and touched the plane of the soul and the higher consciousness of the inner world. But for various reasons which we'll look at in a moment, you couldn't hold that full connection for long. You then fell back into a more ordinary consciousness, and certainly a more difficult consciousness, full of the normal spectrum of emotions and thoughts—the fears, greed's, insecurities, prejudices, reactions, etc., which normally dominate our lives. Much of this is the instinctual-bio-computer programs of our evolution.

What is happening at this point in the Earth's and our evolution is that the human vehicle has reached a sufficient level of development that more of the full consciousness of the soul can be present when we are incarnate. This is referred to as the 'fifth kingdom,' because an entirely new consciousness is becoming manifest on the planet. This means new energies, new ways of perception, new energetic states, and so on. This is a very significant shift, a radical shift. If we look back at the Earth's history, the Earth has evolved four kingdoms. Now the Earth is evolving a fifth. And this fifth kingdom is happening *through* the human kingdom. In the past the plant kingdom built upon the mineral kingdom. Then the animal kingdom emerged out of the plant kingdom. And the human kingdom emerged out of the animal kingdom. Now the kingdom of souls is emerging out of the human kingdom.

This jump is taking place for the Earth as a whole, and therefore for the entirety of humanity. Though we have always had a few individuals who were able to retain soul consciousness while incarnate—these we've recognized as our great geniuses or the spiritually enlightened—they were a rare exception. The vast majority of people lived in the more limited instinctual-based consciousness. Now the Earth is taking this step in the evolution of its consciousness through the human kingdom.

This is called a 'Planetary Initiation.' A Planetary Initiation is when the Earth *as a whole* takes a step in its consciousness, a quantum jump in its evolution. The Earth has taken four Initiations in its evolution, and at each Initiation brought forth a new kingdom: the mineral, plant, animal, and human, and now it's ready to take its fifth Initiation.

As I mentioned previously, this Initiation happens through the human kingdom. That means you and me. Think about that for a moment. In you is happening a vast evolutionary unfoldment. Though we tend to think our spirituality, our personal growth, our issues, and challenges are 'mine,' they are actually the reflection of a vast process at work.

The mechanism through which this happens is via the Antahkarana, the cord that links the soul to the body/personality. The full consciousness of the soul sits in an eighth chakra about one foot above the head. It can be visualized as a sphere of bright light above the head. When you look at a new-born child this direct connection between the soul and the personality is still relatively intact. That is why you see such wisdom in a new born. You see a soul in such purity looking back at you. But very rapidly, due to three factors—the natural turning on of the instincts as the body comes into action, the dense vibrations that the soul encounters upon birth, and the conditioning process that the soul undergoes through interaction with people and life situations—the Antahkarana becomes smaller and the soul consciousness diminishes. Only a very little consciousness comes through it. What comes through primarily is the life energy.

This cord has two components: the life cord and the consciousness cord. In the incarnation and growth process, we 'lose consciousness' and become identified with the body/personality—with the mind, emotions, instincts, and experiences—until we have almost entirely lost contact with soul consciousness. We forget ourselves as souls and come to identify with the body/personality. This is called falling asleep.

But even though the Antahkarana diminishes and our consciousness falls asleep, the cord never disappears. It can be developed and opened. The consciousness of the soul can be re-accessed. That is what any authentic spiritual path is ultimately about. It builds the connection to our soul and a higher force. It builds the Antahkarana.

This process has been always going on for a small number of people. But not the majority. Imagine what would happen when the consciousness cord is built in millions and millions of people. Great numbers of people start waking up to their soul—they start becoming aware of themselves as non-physical spiritual/energetic entities.

It is useful to see it pictorially. Imagine here is the globe of the Earth, and here is a person who builds the bridge from the crown to this sphere of light above her head. She has built her individual Antahkarana and connected to her soul. From the soul there is now a down flow of energy into her body. It can be seen as a bright light that radiates into her and then outwards from her entire aura. Here another person does the same, and another, and another. Many people are becoming bright. Many threads of light are being built into the inner world, and through those threads energy is coming into this world. If you could visualize the Earth as a whole, you would see these threads of energy rising upwards everywhere, and people starting to glow everywhere.

The Planetary Antahkarana

At some point enough threads will have been built, that the *planetary Antahkarana* is built. All these little threads weave together into a larger 'fabric' so to speak—our individual Antahkarana's weave together to form the planetary Antahkarana. A new dimension of connection to the dimension of the soul has been established for the Earth as a whole. And when this connection is built, the 'Earth's Soul' can incarnate another aspect of itself. This is the moment of Planetary Initiation. This is the moment of great awakening which has been foretold by so many mystics down the ages.

The Planetary Initiation can only happen if we make our personal initiation into the connection with our soul. As we build our personal Antahkarana we are building the planetary Antahkarana. We are playing our part in the planet's awakening and initiation.

What seems to be 'my' individual growth process is something much bigger. If we could see from a larger perspective, we would see that each one of us, as individual cells within the planetary entity, is starting to vibrate differently, to enhance and increase its vibration. And this is happening simultaneously to all the cells within the entity that we call the Earth.

It's just like the way spring appears suddenly out of winter. First one sprout shows above ground, then 10, then 1000, then 1,000,000. Many of these human 'cells' are growing threads out of the top of their heads and are linking into the inner world of light around the planet. At some point these threads will reach a critical mass. There will be enough of these threads, and the frequency will have increased enough, that a great opening of energy can happen.

That is the moment of Planetary Initiation. That is the moment when the soul of the Earth can become present in a new way. So in a very real way the work that we are doing as individuals on ourselves has cosmic implications and is bringing something of cosmic proportion. This is what Indigo Souls are really about. You are the souls coming into incarnation as the new energy is emerging. You are the souls who have the evolutionary development to build the Antahkarana. You are the souls through whom the Planetary Initiation is occurring.

Questions & Answers

• *You were talking about the Antahkarana bridge. Is it a good idea to consciously work at building that bridge?*

The more I have gone into inner work, the more that I have come to realize that consciously building the bridge is THE most important part of inner work. Everything else—cleaning up the personality, opening the chakras, etc.,—is a part of the foundation-building work needed so that the bridge can be built. The bridge is built primarily through meditation; it is a deliberate and scientific process. It is because the bridge is built primarily through meditation that I believe that meditation is going to become central for great numbers of people.

There is a second way to build the bridge: through very high levels of thought or feeling in which you begin to access the thoughts and feelings of the soul. That type of thinking or feeling can be summed up under the words 'aspiration' or 'inspiration.' When we begin to try and sense the higher forces, the higher intelligence, the higher blueprint, we are sending streams of energy up the Antahkarana and we are accessing levels of thought and feeling of the soul itself. I am thinking of those of you who are teachers. The way you can present certain material and provoke certain thinking processes in your students will contribute to building the Antahkarana.

Also the feeling of love is a vibration that lifts us up?

Exactly, that is the feeling level of it. Love is the feeling level that builds the bridge. Both feeling and thought can build that bridge.

• *When you said "we are formed out of conflicting forces" like various entities and cosmic forces and the inner plane and things that are being stepped down, I wondered if the conflicts I am feeling all result from my childhood and past lives, or if they are created on a much bigger level?*

My understanding is that this is the root cause of our inner conflicts, that we are composed literally of different streams of energy and entities. That our physical, emotional, and mental bodies are composed of different entities.

You mean that the mental body is one entity, and the emotional body is another entity, and there is a fight going on?

Exactly.

And I am the battlefield?

Yes, you have got it. What they say in esotericism is that the coming together of these different entities and forces on the earth is literally a battleground. That the Earth is a kind of cosmic battleground of various forces. That the good guys aren't always winning. And that some of these battles and struggles are taking place in our own psyches and bodies. When I used to listen to Christianity, I used to roll my eyes when people would talk about the devil and say things like "Oh, the devil this, or the devil made me do it."

But as I started to understand esotericism, a whole new insight opened up about this. The word 'devil' has its roots in the Sanskrit word *deva*. *Devas* are non-physical entities that live on other planes of existence that interpenetrate with our plane. Some of these *devas* are bright and light, and some are dark and dangerous. Some of them operate through certain kinds of emotions and thought patterns. You can feel some of these darker spirits if you go into certain types of low-life bars, or sometimes in the train stations, where there are down-and-out people who these spirits have entered.

You may be familiar with the Great Invocation from Bailey where he says, "May Light and Love and Power seal the door where evil dwells." As I have gone deeper into meditation and consciousness, I have become aware of those doors as they live in me and as they live in others. I can feel these 'chained entities,' for that is the best way to describe them, that are imprisoned and chained inside of these doors, but are very real living forces in us. I am aware of certain moments, sometimes when I am tired or in pain or upset, where these entities can squeeze a little bit out of the door. Or if I get hurt and emotional and reactive, that in certain moments they lash and roar.

• *I have the feeling that not only is the Antahkarana built from our side, but also from the other side, from the soul downwards towards the personality. I especially feel it going on sometimes at night.*

In the earlier stages of human development, the consciousness was almost completely wrapped in the density of emotions and thoughts of the lower centers. There was very little longing from the personality side for the soul. The building of the Antahkarana came almost entirely from the soul as it tried to penetrate through to the personality. You may have noticed one form of this, as the subtle inner voice of guidance. Gradually certain developments take place within the personality and a 'reaching upwards,' or aspiration starts occurring in various steps and stages. Then it becomes a two-way process, with you doing work from the personality towards the soul, and the soul working from above downwards towards the personality. At a certain point, the 'connection' is built enough that there is almost a constant communication of energies back and forth.

• *I feel slightly overwhelmed by this big picture! And on the other hand I feel a joy. I feel a happiness to feel I am in all this and a part of what is going on.*

It reminds me of moments when, shall we say, my 'horizons expanded' and I began to see a bigger sense of things. Sometimes I was just overwhelmed by a sense of being insignificant. It would be kind of devastating to my ego! I liked to feel important, and special, and all those good things. But at other times I had exactly the opposite feeling. I felt, "Wow, my personality is just a faint shadow. The real me is big and vast—this is a big thing that's happening here! How great to be a part of this vast Cosmos. I'm sure glad Existence created me!"

And when I feel this, I feel as if I have existed from the very beginning, I have a sense that 'I' as an entity was created when Existence was created and I have been here ever since. And I have a sense that I will be here till the very end, unfolding more and more divinity.

About the Authors

Kabir Jaffe

Kabir is an American who has spent the past 35 years involved in inner work. Eighteen of those years were spent in an ashram in India, living with the Indian mystic Osho, exploring eastern mystic traditions and meditation. Kabir is a psychologist with extensive training in Humanistic and Transpersonal Psychology, an astrologer, and the founder of Essence Training and the International University of Consciousness and Inner Sciences.

Kabir is a scientist of consciousness, a visionary, and a futurist. He is a guide for people on the path of inner development, as well as a trainer of professionals for working with others. His work with energy and consciousness is a unique blend of science and spirituality, combining cutting edge science and ancient wisdom teachings into a dynamic and experiential methodology for the art of conscious living and walking the Path in the 21st century.

Ritama Davidson

Ritama was born in Curacao, Netherlands Antilles, in the Caribbean and spent her teenage years in Europe. She graduated from the Theater School in Amsterdam in modern dance and choreography and worked as a professional dancer and choreographer. She later studied Shiatsu with Ohashi in New York and graduated from the Florida School of Massage. She was in private practice for 15 years as a body-oriented therapist. Her later studies include extensive training in energy and chakra work, and in Humanistic Psychologically-oriented Therapy—Family Therapy, Voice Dialogue, and Psychodrama. She has been involved in practices of meditation and spirituality since 1979. Ritama has been leading groups along with Kabir in North and South America and in Europe for the past 10 years.

The Essence Training Institute

✦

Training for Adult Indigos

Programs in Energy, Inner Work, and the New Consciousness

Would you like to learn more about Indigos?

Would you like to take your next steps upon the Path?

Essence Training is an Inner Work School for people who want to:

> Explore themselves
> Share with others of like spirit
> Take significant steps towards fulfilling the purpose you have come for
> Build your Antahkarana
> Learn to use energy for living and spiritual development
> Play a more active part in the unfolding evolutionary events

Programs held internationally.

Contact us if this material has interested you and you would like to sponsor talks or workshops by an Essence Trainer in your area.

For more information
www.essencetraining.com
info@essencetraiing.com

APPENDIX

Are you an Indigo Soul?

✦

Some common characteristics of Indigo Souls

Indigo Souls:

- Are highly intelligent though they may not express it in 'normal' ways.

- Are creative and enjoy making things.

- Need to understand—always asking why, especially when asked to do something.

- May have difficulties in school with control, repetitious learning, etc.

- Often rebellious and resist authority, though they might not dare to express it.

- Have trouble with systems they consider broken or ineffective, i.e., political, educational, medical, and legal.

- Are often angry if they feel their rights are being taken away. They may oscillate between fear and fury at 'Big Brother watching you.'

- Feel a burning desire to do something to change and improve the world. May be stymied in what they do. Many have trouble identifying their Path.

- Are frustrated with or reject the traditional American dream—9-5 career, marriage, 2.5 children, house with white picket fence, etc.

- Are alienated from or angry with politics—the feeling that your voice won't count and that the outcome really doesn't matter.

- May have felt existential depression, despair, and helplessness, and may suffer with the question "Why am I here?"

- Are unhappy with mundane, menial jobs, especially in hierarchical authority structures.

- Prefer cooperative efforts, leadership positions, or working alone.

- Are deeply empathic with others but are often intolerant of stupidity.

- Maybe extremely emotionally sensitive including crying at the drop of a hat, (no shielding) or maybe the opposite and show no expression of emotion (full shielding).

- May have trouble with RAGE.

- Have psychic or spiritual interests while fairly young.

- Had few if any Indigo role models.

- Have strong intuition.

- Have random behavior pattern or mind styles (symptoms of Attention Deficit Disorder), may have trouble focusing on assigned tasks, may jump around in conversations.

- May have had psychic experiences, such as premonitions, seeing angels or ghosts, out of body experiences, hearing voices.

- May be electrically disruptive, such as watches not working in their presence, electrical equipment malfunctioning, and lights blowing out. May be disturbed by electrical radiations. And/or may be addicted to electrical vibrations (computer, TV, cell phone).

- Are highly sexually expressive and inventive or may reject sexuality in boredom; may explore alternate types of sexuality.

- May carry a strong intention to achieve higher spiritual connection.

- Seek meaning to their life and understanding about the world. May seek this through religion or spirituality, spiritual groups and books, experimentation with drugs, sex, self-help groups, and books.

(Adopted from Wendy Chapman)

Chapman, W. (2001). 'Are You An Adult Indigo?' from Metagifted Education Resource Organization website,www.metagifted.org: http://www.metagifted.org/topics/metagifted/indigo/adultIndigos/areYouAnAdultIndigo.html

978-0-595-36692-7
0-595-36692-9

Made in the USA